From Glass to Glass

A Rugby League Journey

Paul Loughlin

with Andrew Quirke

London League Publications Ltd

From Grass to Glass

A Rugby League Journey

© Paul Loughlin and Andrew Quirke. Foreword © Bernard Dwyer.

The moral right of Paul Loughlin and Andrew Quirke to be identified as the authors has been asserted.

Cover design © Stephen McCarthy.

Front cover: Paul Loughlin before the 1988 Great Britain Lions tour to Australia (Photo: Brian Peers). Back cover: Celebrating another triumph with St Helens, the 1993 Premiership Final success at Old Trafford. (Photo: *St Helens Reporter*)

All photographs in this book are from private collections unless otherwise credited. No copyright has been intentionally breached; please contact London League Publications Ltd if you believe there has been a breach of copyright.

A CIP catalogue record for this book is available from the British Library.

First published in Great Britain in August 2011 by:
London League Publications Ltd, P.O. Box 65784, London NW2 9NS

ISBN: 978-1903659-56-4

Cover design by: Stephen McCarthy Graphic Design
                            46, Clarence Road, London N15 5BB

Layout: Peter Lush

Printed and bound in Great Britain by Charlesworth Press, Wakefield

I would like to dedicate this book to my family for their support through the years, and to my step dad Paul Burns who passed away in 1999; he was a good mate, my buddy and is still missed.

I would also like to thank Andrew and Peter for their time and commitment to this book.

Foreword

I remember the first time I went down to Saints as a 16-year-old. I had been asked to go by Bob Dagnall and Johnny Fishwick; they had been watching me play. I was invited to train with the Colts. I went for my first training session and there was one lad who stood out from all the rest. I don't know if it was because of his passing ability, his long, striding breaks or his striking resemblance to the keyboard player from Sparks. He had his wedge hairstyle and his tache. I learnt that his name was Paul Loughlin. Lockers was outstanding. I was trying to impress so thought I would have him during a game of tick-and-pass. I chased him all over the pitch and never got near him. He was that good; I kept getting a big right-handed hand-off on my nose. I thought "this kid's got something about him".

I've known him for nearly 30 years from that day; he's been an absolute pleasure to have as a mate. He became an outstanding player; some people don't give him the credit for how good he really was. He overcame a host of injury problems too. He's never too serious off the pitch, usually has his tongue firmly in his cheek and is one of the funniest people I've ever met in my life.

I got to know Paul really well during our time at Bradford. We'd had some nights out during our time at Saints, saw each other in training and got on well but there was a full squad of us there together. We started rooming together at Bradford and we got to know each other better personally. We got into a little bit of bother from time to time but Paul was always entertaining. I'd be lying on the bed; Lockers would go into the toilet. A few minutes later, he would reappear stark naked walking around like someone from John Cleese's Ministry of Funny Walks. Typical of his sometimes random, bizarre humour. Every day with Lockers was an experience. He was just a funny bloke to be with and you can't take him seriously for one minute.

He's been on two Lions tours, and has plenty of tales to tell. He's a likeable man. I've never known anyone have a bad word to say about him. If you've met Lockers, he's a cracking bloke and he's your mate. I appreciate the opportunity to provide the foreword for his book and feel honoured to do so.

Bernard Dwyer
May 2011

Paul and Andrew Quirke at a meeting to discuss this book.
(Photo: Peter Lush)

My work on this book is dedicated to the memory of Emma Ratcliffe who died at the age of 27 in March 2011. Emma was a big Saints fan and an inspiration to those who knew her with her joy for life Personally, she gave me great encouragement about this project and my other books. She will be sadly missed.

I would also like to dedicate my work on this book to Oliver with all my love.

I would like to thank Tommy Frodsham, Chris Gill, Sprayhurst Social Club, Ben Smithurst, Kevin Gill, Paul Bennett, Claire Horton, Mike Appleton at St Helens RLFC, Mick Scott and Sarah at Halifax RLFC, Deb Townsend at Widnes RLFC Museum, Bill Bates, Peter Lush and Dave Farrar from London League Publications Ltd, everyone who graciously gave their time to be interviewed and most of all Paul Loughlin for giving him the opportunity to work on this book with him, it's been a privilege.

Andrew Quirke
May 2011

London League Publications Ltd would like to thank Michael O'Hare for sub-editing the book with his usual skill and patience; Steve McCarthy for designing the cover; Brian Peers, Bernard Platt, Andrew Varley, Dave Williams & Sig Kasatkin, the *St Helens Reporter*, the *St Helens Star* and Alex Service for helping with the photographs and the staff of Charlesworth Press for printing it.

Peter Lush and Dave Farrar

Contents

1.	Early years	1
2.	Joining Saints	9
3.	Alex Murphy in charge	25
4.	Mike McClennan arrives	43
5.	Final days at Saints	59
6.	Great Britain	67
7.	Off to Odsal	81
8.	Wembley finals	97
9.	Huddersfield	109
10.	Swinton	113
11.	On the groundstaff	117
12.	Reflections	121
	Appendix: Statistics and records	136

With Lisa.

With Lisa, Millie and Tom on holiday in Turkey in 2010.

1. Early years

My rugby story with St Helens RLFC began in 1983. Back then just as the coal and glass industries had sustained the town in better times; the star-studded power of the Saints side had flickered then died. Now the team represented the town: young men looking to make a life for themselves without the necessary resources to be truly successful. These were hard times for both club and town alike. With high unemployment and little in the way of leisure, Saints offered an escape for the supporters and players. Saints were, and still are, the focal point of the town. We were fearless though and had a lot of fun along the way. Looking back, my personal journey was incredible. I entered the game as a part-time player scoring three-point tries in winter rugby and I left the game a man who had represented his country and a full-time rugby league professional in the summer era. I still hold the most-goals- and most-points-in-a-game records at St Helens RLFC. I played with or against all the top players in British rugby league between 1983 and 2000. I played in Wembley Challenge Cup Finals five times and ended up winning the Super League with Bradford Bulls. This is a tale of beers, great friends and good laughs. I am Paul Loughlin and this is my story.

* * * * * *

I was born Paul John Patrick Loughlin on 28 July 1966 at Whiston Hospital. I've got a twin sister Marie, a younger sister Julie and my younger brother Mike.

With Marie and I being twins, we shared the weight out between us and were around seven pounds each at birth. I was the smallest as my youngest sister Julie was nearly 10 pounds when she was born. Marie was always taller than me and it took me until when I was about 13 before I started really growing. I was tall but skinny - like Rodders from *Only Fools and Horses* - until I was 21.

Paddy Loughlin (Paul's dad)
"My grandfather was from Galway and was six foot five which was a great height in those days. He came over to England around 1908. He was from a landed family. He is the one that we all get the height from. I remember he always had a flat cap on and had a big

1

moustache. He didn't really say much, mind you we're a bit like that when we go out. We only start talking after the fourth pint. My mother's side is the Collins family, her brother, Bob Collins, was a bookie. He had played professional football for Wigan Athletic before the war in the Third Division North."

My happiest memories growing up were playing outside; especially football in the park with my friends. We used to be told off by the neighbours for playing football in the street with the ball banging against their wall. You don't seem to see kids playing outside as much these days. We had to really because we didn't have the technology that kids have to entertain themselves with today. We just made our own fun. I remember playing at my Nan's in Pewfall or my other Nan's in Thatto Heath; in their back garden playing rugby games on my own. I used plant pots if there was no paper to make a ball with. I would have a cricket ball and bat and play test matches on my own. I think people my age always look back and remember it being red hot in the summer and freezing cold with snow in the winter.

I used to have a surgical shoe because my right foot was bending in; I had to have it straightened. I was always having trouble when I was little. I got my leg caught in a tram in Blackpool and twisted it when I was six. I had burst blood vessels in my thigh. I had to be treated with a black tar like substance smeared over my leg. My leg ballooned and I nearly lost it. Fortunately, I recovered.

When I was young and lived on Rivington Road, my mum and I used to walk to my Nan's in Thatto Heath. As we passed the Knowsley Road ground, I would tell my mum that when I signed for Saints, I would buy her a sports car and a fur coat. If I had saved up all my career, I wouldn't have been able to have afforded them. Later on I remember trying to climb over the fence at Knowsley Road to try and watch the 'A' team.

My dad Terry had played for Saints in the 1960s after being banned *sine die* at Salford, and later for Blackpool Borough. He jokes that's why I was taught to play rugby properly and not his dirty habits. He was a prop forward and is better known as Paddy.

Paddy Loughlin
"I got the nickname 'Paddy' at school and since then we've had dogs called Paddy, parrots called Paddy and now a grandchild called Paddy."

2

I went to St Teresa's School in St Helens, but I was always into football. It was only when another lad at the school, Dave Lee, who was the brother of professional rugby league player Mark, asked me to come and play rugby with them that I got started. I told him that I would have a game although I didn't know the rules. Believe it or not, I was the fastest at the school. They put me on the wing and I raced in for five tries in my first game. They had to show me where the tryline was and yell at me to stop before I ran out of play ball in hand, a la Forrest Gump in the movie.

I went on from there and quickly found that I loved the game. My headmaster was a man called Brian Higgins; he was a Widnes fan and rugby mad. There was another teacher called Peter Atherton who was keen on rugby. St Teresa's always had good rugby teams and I ended up getting picked for the team the year above me. The year after, I was team captain. Following on from that, I got into the St Helens town team which I also captained. When I was about 10, my mum, my sisters and I all joined Ruskin Park Running Club which I also enjoyed.

Paddy Loughlin

"When Paul first asked me to take him training in rugby league, I'd only seen him play rugby union at school. He was outstanding at school. I recall the headmaster ringing me asking whether I would give Paul permission to play for the school team as he was three years too young. He wasn't a big lad, he was tall but all kneecaps and boots. He just had natural skills with his handling and so on. He could always kick a ball. He had been kicking a ball since he could walk. He used to drive everybody bloody mad by kicking goals against the side of the house. Thatto Heath School gave Paul an award for being the best player in town."

I used to go to watch Saints with my dad. Eric Chisnall was one of my heroes as a kid. Saints had a good side at the time with the likes of George Nicholls, Geoff Pimblett and Roy Matthias. Eric stood out because he never seemed to miss a game. There was a surprise party for Eric recently because he had been involved with Saints for 40 years. He was a big bloke which helped him stand out to me too. He would always make half breaks and was quick for a big bloke.

When I moved to West Park School aged 11, they only played union so I drifted away from league. People always think of St Helens as a rugby league-mad town, which it is, but there were some schools that didn't play the sport until the past couple of decades. I played rugby union for Merseyside Schools with Paul Hulme who went to Wade Deacon School in Widnes. My mum and dad split up when I was 12 and I moved to Ashton with my mum so I didn't go to Saints as much. My dad was coaching UGB at the time and they would organise coach trips to the big games which I would go on.

My first sip of beer was when Saints played Leeds in the 1978 Challenge Cup Final. I was there watching with my dad. My dad took me on the train. It looked like his bag contained about 48 cans of McEwan's Bitter. I was only 12; I had a sip out of one of his cans but said that I didn't like it. He told me I was a good lad; I reckon he was pleased he didn't have to share them with me. That was the year Derek Noonan knocked on near the line at the end of the game and Saints fans blamed him for the defeat with the phrase "Noonan's got no fingers". I've watched it on television since and I don't think it was a clear cut chance. The cover was coming across to get him. It was unfortunate he got tagged with that because he was a good player.

Bob Dagnall and Johnny Fishwick ran the Colts side at Saints along with Jeff Heaton and Billy Appleton and his dad who followed all Saints teams everywhere. With my dad, they got an under-17s team together called the Hare and Hounds. They were based at Saints and it was only when I joined them that I started to play and watch league again. I had missed it.

There were a lot of good lads in the same position, players who loved league but had been unable to play it because of the school they attended. There was Dave Lee and Shaun Allen. Shaun and I signed for Saints from the Hare and Hounds side. The year after, Bernard Dwyer came from Hare and Hounds too. Without that junior side, I don't think I would have ended up playing rugby league.

It was around this time I had my first proper drink, I was about 16. A couple of lads I used to knock about with took me to a pub in Ashton. The landlord didn't seem bothered about us being under age; we would sit in the back room playing pool. We would get half a mild because it was the cheapest thing, it was about 15p at the time. It wasn't like today where you get kids drinking bottles of cider in the park. Some of these kids today can sup more than grown men. Although my first drink was at 16, possibly later than a lot of other kids, I've made up for it since.

A family group: my mum Christine and dad Paddy with Julie, me and Marie.

I wasn't very good at school; I didn't do very well at my exams and took a job painting and decorating. Unfortunately, that didn't last long and once I started playing rugby, I wanted to try and make it as a player. In the early 1980s growing up in St Helens, there were very few jobs. Playing rugby was probably my only way to make a living.

I remember watching the 1982 Challenge Cup semi-final between Widnes and Leeds. The Widnes player Mick Adams hit the crossbar with a kick and Keiron O'Loughlin regathered to score. There was a huge crowd on that day and I was part of it. I remember thinking "this is what I want to be" - I never thought I would make it though.

I remember being at my Nan's and my dad phoned me saying that Oldham wanted to sign me. Frankie Barrow, who is my godfather, was Oldham coach at the time and wanted to sign me on my 17th birthday. I was really excited, but my dad told me to hang on. He phoned round a few people and Saints said they would have a look at me first. My dad rang me back and told me that Saints wanted to sign me; I would have signed for them for nothing. It's a good job my dad wouldn't have let me.

I went down to the club with my dad and he helped sort a contract out for me although it wasn't a contract as such. In those days, when you signed, you signed for life, it wasn't a fixed term. I think I am right in recalling that £3,000 per year was the amount I signed for with bonuses for appearing for Lancashire, Great Britain under-21s and the Great Britain side itself. Little did I know at the time that I would manage to appear for all of them before I was 21.

Paddy Loughlin

"He played in the under-17s alongside the likes of Sean Allen who had already unofficially signed for Saints. You all knew who had been signed up and who hadn't. I looked at him and realised he was doing really well. As the season progressed, he got a bit better.

The next season, he went in for the Lancashire trials. Sean Allen was stand-off in one team with Paul at centre. One coach came up to me and asked, "Who is the lad in the centre?" I told him he was Paul Loughlin. He replied "That's what your name is". I explained that Paul was my son; the coach asked why I hadn't pushed him? I said that it wasn't my job to push him, it was his job as selector and that the team should be selected on what he saw not on who people were. Paul got picked for Lancashire."

After playing amateur rugby league for Lancashire, he got picked for the international side but didn't want to go. I had to ask Bob Dagnall and Johnny Fishwick to have a word with him. I knew if they spoke to him, there was a chance he might listen.

Saints then gave Paul a trial in the 'A' team, but played him on the wing. I didn't know anything about it and went mad when I found out. He shouldn't have played on the wing, that wasn't his position. If they wanted to see what he could do, they should have played him at centre. The point is if you get offered a trial and don't play in your position, then you don't perform to the level the club has heard you can and so you don't get signed up. I wouldn't let Paul play another trial. I told Saints if they wanted him, they would have to sign him. I thought he would go all the way."

I never thought I was that good before professional clubs became interested in me. I didn't think I was up to that level. I've always felt that I've lacked a bit of confidence in my own ability. When Saints came in for me, I was overjoyed and couldn't believe it. I was a fan of the club and it just meant the world to me. It was something I had always wanted to do but never thought I could achieve, it felt like all my Christmases had come at once. The moment where I signed my contract for Saints was probably the best moment I ever had. I felt like I had already made it. I didn't have a mobile then and thinking back, I don't think we had a house phone at the time. I felt like nipping to local journalist Ronnie Barker's house and getting him to put it in the *St Helens Star* for me, I wanted everybody to know.

I signed for Saints in 1983 and the club was in a rebuilding phase. They had signed Steve Rule, a full-back from Salford, but he was on his last legs really. Mel James had been a good player, but was on his way out. A lot of the older players like Roy Matthias were packing in. Barrie Ledger was making a name for himself on the wing, Roy Haggerty was at centre. Shaun Allen was the other centre. There was a good pack with Paul Forber, Graham Liptrot, and Harry Pinner. The half-backs were any two from Neil Holding, Chris Arkwright and Steve Peters. Chris Arkwright in particular was someone I looked up to because of the way he played.

We were local lads too, except Tony Burke who travelled from Bramley in Yorkshire, Peter Gorley who travelled from Cumbria and Clive Griffiths who was Welsh. The rest of us were from St Helens and it's becoming like that again with the present Saints side, which I think is good. The club was rebuilding after the successes of the 1970s. We never seemed to win anything after 1976. They were barren years until Mal Meninga's arrival in 1984. A lot of teams struggled in the early 1980s, including Wigan. The top sides were the two Hull teams and Widnes.

St Teresa's Primary School with a five-trophy haul in 1977. Paul Loughlin (holding rugby ball) captained the side. Paul Wellens' brother Ian is third from the left in the front row; Mark Lee (St Helens and Salford) is on the far right. Another former Saint, Paul Round, is first on the left in the middle row. (Courtesy Alex Service)

Early triumph at Knowsley Road: Receiving the Pilkington Sevens Trophy on behalf of St Teresa's Primary School from David Pilkington.

2. Joining Saints

I was so excited at joining Saints aged only 17. I remember my first training session at the club. I got the bus from Ashton to Boundary Road where Saints used to train on a big Astroturf pitch. I walked into the Boundary Road facility and there were two dressing rooms, one for the first team and one for the Colts, 'A' teamers and trialists. I walked into the first team dressing room unwittingly and was greeted with the words "I think you'll be in that one lad" accompanied with a hand pointing back the way I came.

It was the same at Knowsley Road as well; the away dressing room was for the 'A' team lads. You had to earn your right to get changed in the home dressing room - it was right too.

It could be quite painful training on Astroturf; players were getting sprains and strains. My problem when I joined Saints was shin splints. I was out for six months before I had even played my first game. I had to have cortisone injections in my legs. There was no give in the Astroturf. We didn't do stuff on the floor there; it was more fitness and ball skills with the more physical stuff being done at the club.

It was a bit difficult fitting into the Saints dressing room at first; there were so many big personalities. New players earned respect by doing well for the side. The other players watched who was going to be signed. Newcomers had to train hard, do well, and take their chance. Then when they made it into the first team, not try to be one of the lads straight away, it was better to blend in and stay in the background. It's probably easier for players today as the first team trains with the younger players anyway. Back then, the teams were separate and it was tougher to fit in when you made the step up. A youngster would wait for the established first-teamers to put their bag down then take whatever spot there was left, usually near the door.

I would play for the Colts on a Saturday, the 'A' team played on a Friday night. There would be two substitute places to play for in the first team on a Sunday. There would also be two places on 'the panel': those players didn't play but were travelling reserves and got a bit of extra money.

There were quality players in all the 'A' teams back then. Johnny 'Miffer' Smith would always seem to get one of the first-team sub spots, I thought possibly because he was best mates with Graham Liptrot. Paul Forber generally got the other spot.

I started off playing centre in the under-17s, but I used to like playing full-back because I could learn the game from that position, especially when I had good players in front of me. When Steve Rule was finishing at Saints and prior to Phil Veivers arriving I had a few first team games at full-back, sharing the position with Kevin Wellens. I dropped down into the 'A' team some weekends. The 'A' team included players such as Brian Parkes, Mick Bowes, Dennis Litherland and Mick Glover. They had been first-team regulars and so were great to learn from. I had a few games at centre in the first team, started enjoying it and it took off from there. It took a while to feel properly established in the Saints side. It was hard to progress through the ranks back then. I had to learn my trade in the 'A' team. There were some quality players in the 'A' team and establishing yourself in that side wasn't easy. They were all fighting for a place on the panel there. The 'A' team matches were rock hard, it wasn't like the Academy today. There were plenty of experienced players involved.

Swinton always had a good 'A' team. Widnes and Wigan would have international quality players in their 'A' teams. One visit to Central Park for an 'A' team game saw Eric Hughes tackle Joe Lydon very hard. Players such as Shaun Wane were coming through for Wigan. I found that some 'A' team games were more physical than first team games. I saw players get some terrible injuries at that level such as when Colin McIntyre broke his jaw.

Even testimonial matches were seen as a chance to get into the first team. They weren't as fast as a first-team game, but were certainly as ferocious. It was a great preparation and meant youngsters were more battle-hardened and ready for first-team rugby when their chance did come. There wasn't much money about and no guaranteed contract money so it was a desperate battle for that £25 extra appearance money. It was brutal.

I made my first-team debut for Saints against Oldham as a sub on 1 April 1984 at Knowsley Road. I got the bus from Ashton to the Saints ground. I put my bag down and realised I had forgotten to bring my boots. I was panicking, trying to work out what I should do. The kitman at the time was Eric Leach who was the most respected man at the club, as most kit men are.

Barrie Ledger was sitting beside me and I told him of my predicament. He started laughing and told me to go and see Eric as he had lots of spare boots. Eric walked in, puffing on a huge cigar, he said: "Now then Lock, are you looking forward to your debut?" I told him that I was, but that I had left my boots at home and needed a pair. He told me to stand up, weighed me up then told me to wait. He came back with a pair of boots that must have been dropped off by a clown from a passing circus. They were huge, size 13, maybe John Mantle's old boots. I was too scared to say anything. I started to get my kit on and thought I had better try the boots on. There was an acre of space at the front of each boot; I thought there was no way I could play in them. Barrie Ledger advised me to get a pair of spare socks, roll them in a ball and shove them at the space at the front of each boot. I did this but they were still a bit loose. Barry then advised me to tie the laces of the boots as tight as possible. At this point, the boots finally felt OK. I was on the bench, and as I was warming up, my feet started tingling a little bit. Twenty minutes into the game, my feet started going numb. I thought that I had better keep running up and down the touchline, I must have looked stupid constantly running. Half-time came, I didn't get a shout to go on. I told Barrie I was losing the feeling in my feet and he couldn't stop laughing.

With 20 minutes to go, I was brought on to replace Clive Griffiths – by this point I couldn't feel my feet at all. As soon as I got on, Saints got a penalty. Harry Pinner shouted me over, "Come here, young 'un, can you kick this?" It was about 40 yards out. Eager to impress, I told him I would have a go.

I put the ball down, took three steps back, boom. It sailed over and I never felt a thing in my feet. First touch of the ball, first points for the club. It was *Roy of the Rovers* stuff to me. Even better, I got the feeling back in my feet about two weeks later. I gave Eric Leach the boots back and never forgot my own pair again.

Barrie Ledger

"My first impression on meeting Paul was that he was a young, shy lad. I could see he had potential from watching him play for the Colts. His strength as a player was his size. He was a clever player really although he wasn't the quickest. He was very good with his hands.

He was a very funny, dry lad. He used to come out with some cracking one-liners. He was quiet at first but once he settled in he was fine. He came into his own."

My first full game was against Widnes on 23 April. I looked in the programme to see who I would be marking. I had to mark Eddie Cunningham and Eric Hughes, two noted hard men of the game. As a 17-year-old, it was daunting, particularly when another player seemed to take an instant dislike to me. They were a quality side with stars such as Joe Lydon. Cunningham and Hughes seemed to take it easy on me at first, but they soon changed their minds. It was hard to get used to the pace of the game.

Paddy Loughlin

"When he got into the first team at first, there were some comments about his passing to his winger. I told them not to worry and that it would all come together with experience."

I also learnt not to run straight at people. Another Lancashire club later signed the player who didn't like me. He must have looked at my name on the team-sheet and thought it was Christmas because he always seemed to tackle me high. You seemed to be able to get away with high tackles more back then. I talked to my dad about it as I was fed up of getting my nose smashed. He advised me that when this player had the ball I was to rattle him. I ended up practising stiff arms in my Nan's back garden with my dad. My dad had been an old-school prop forward so knew how to dish out the rough stuff. After about half an hour, he had nearly broken my ribs four times.

Paddy Loughlin

"I had done so many daft things in my playing career, it resulted in me seeing plenty of clean water as I was generally first in the bath! My record was seven minutes at Workington, the guy in the changing rooms hadn't even run the bath, he was surprised. We had this thing that Paul wouldn't follow that path and would be a clean footballer.

Early in Paul's career, he was having problems with another player. I told Paul straight, he was going to have to give him some back otherwise he would murder him every time because he would think he was an easy mark. Paul gave him a crack during a game and I asked him how his opponent had reacted. He said he had told him, 'good tackle'. I replied, 'Aye, well watch for him next time.'"

We then played this player's club in a night match and I told Barrie I was going to sort him out. The first time I had the ball, he hit me high as usual. I waited for him to take the ball in and hit him across the face, splitting his nose. I was shouting to Barrie, "I've done him, I've done him, it will all stop now." It didn't stop, if anything, it got worse.

The referees let you get away with a bit more at this time. Fred Lindop was coming to the end of his career and Stan Wall and John Holdsworth were among the leading referees. They made sure the game wasn't about them. There are some good referees today but I always refer back to the likes of Holdsworth as 'proper refs'. None of the players would give them stick. I very rarely got in trouble with the officials though.

I was sent off at Saints once, got sinbinned twice and got sent off once while at Bradford. Like I say, we used to be able to get away with a bit more and some of the players today might have struggled with some of the rough stuff that was around in the 1980s. I used to like playing rugby though and used to leave the tough play to the likes of Arkie, Roundy and Forber. Steve Peters was another tough, good, skilful player. It was difficult for him to secure a regular place though because of the half-backs we had at the club.

Harry Pinner was captain when I was coming into the side. He was coming to the end of his time at the club. I remember one home game against Wigan; it was a very tight game. I flew out of the line in defence leaving a gap for them to go through and score. Harry railroaded me like a teacher telling someone off. It was right in front of a packed corner of the Popular Side of the ground. I felt about four inches tall and just wanted to disappear. I just nodded and kept apologising. He was a good player though, a superb ball-handler.

As for cementing my position in the side, I did play full-back for Great Britain Colts in 1984-85 and later played there for the full Great Britain side on tour against New Zealand. It was a position I was comfortable in. Back then, teams would always go for a big kick on the last tackle and with my 'Dobbin' kick I was ideal. I preferred centre in the end though as I think you can get away with not having lightning pace at centre but you can't at full-back. Having said that, there have been some great full-backs who didn't have blistering pace. Phil Veivers was one because his positional play was so good. Paul Wellens is another one; he reads the game so well he is one of the best full-backs there has ever been at Saints.

Great Britain Colts squad 1984–85.

Goalkicking is something that can keep you in a team especially if you are struggling for form. I enjoyed it when I was putting them over though. I went to UGB[1] when my dad was coach there and I once kicked a goal from the halfway line when I was about 10 or 11. I used to practice goalkicking when I was young over the 'Sidney Street' sign where we lived. It eventually takes its' toll on you though. I constantly tore my abductor muscles through goalkicking. If you ask most goalkickers, they will tell you it eventually takes its toll on your body. I stopped goalkicking because I was getting groin pulls. If you are not striking the ball well, they are not going to go over. Of course, for the first part of my career I was kicking in mud which made it harder. Goalkicking has changed. When I came into the game, you would dig a little hole for the ball with your heel. Then came perching the ball on top of a pile of sand and now there are specially designed kicking tees. Goalkickers have it easy today with kicking tees and a fantastic standard of pitches, I don't know how they ever miss these days. There's still a fine art to it though. I could kick goals from a long way and it came in handy for the side.

Billy Benyon and Peter Gartland were my first coaches at Saints. Billy had become first team coach in May 1982. Peter was Billy's assistant and ran the 'A' team. Billy was already a legend at Saints because he had enjoyed a long playing career at the club and gained international honours. He was renowned as a tough man. I found him to be a nice guy. Don't get me wrong, he did have a hard side when

---

[1] An amateur club based in St Helens

things weren't going well. He gave me my chance in the first team which is something I will never forget.

On a Tuesday night Billy would have us doing laps of the pitch. After six laps, he would order us to speed it up. You would get to 10 laps and be absolutely shattered. I heard another player gasp "Wait till Billy joins in." At first, I couldn't understand what he meant. All of a sudden, Billy's tracksuit top would come off and he would start sprinting alongside us with his dodgy arm pumping away. "Don't stop till you've got past me" he'd say and off he would race, fresh as a daisy. Billy was fit as a fiddle; he would get to the front of the pack then open up a gap. We would be on our 20th lap; on our hands and knees trying to catch him. Our legs would turn to jelly and I used to fervently hope that he wouldn't turn up each Tuesday. Our forwards were pretty fit, although Roy Haggerty was most effective in short bursts. The likes of Arkie, Platty and Tony Burke were very fit though. They could run forever.

There was never any weight training or fitness coaches when I started in the game. Andy Platt started to use it though and he got a few others interested. I remember walking into the Old Road Labour Club shortly after signing for Saints with my club vest on. All the old fellas in there were Wiganers. I walked in one hot afternoon for a glass of pop and was met with "Where's tha been?" I told them that I had been training for Saints. One replied "Tha's got shoulders like a sauce bottle." That helped me make my mind up to start weight training. I used to go with Andy Platt to a gym in Wigan to try to become a bit bigger.

Thursday night at the club was touch-and-pass which everybody enjoyed. We all really looked forward to that. You can learn things from touch-and-pass such as how to run into gaps and passing both ways. After that, the coach would pick his team for the weekend and you would run through some moves.

Then there would be a Saturday morning session but, being honest, I think that was just to blow the cobwebs off those of us who had overdone it on the Friday night. The training back then was nothing like it is today.

When the young players were travelling reserve for a game, we would have to rub the first-teamers down. There were players like Mal Meninga whose legs were massive, it would take ages. Then there were Burke, Arkwright, Round, Forber and Platt. All had huge tree trunk like legs. I would feel like I'd been in a game myself when I'd got through that lot. Then Liptrot would get on, but he wouldn't get off. There would be two of us with a leg each and he would be doing commentary saying, "It's Paul in the lead". If you weren't rubbing hard enough, he would complain "I'm going to be spinning round on one leg". He'd stay for ages; we would be dripping with sweat after rubbing down all the other players, sitting in our shorts because it was so hot, rubbing oil into him.

Sometimes Lippy would fall asleep, usually after we had done his neck and his back. The only thing we wouldn't do for him is his belly and I'm glad because it would have taken ages. He was a brave bloke though and came back from an incredible four broken jaws. At training, nobody could beat him at short sprints over 20 yards although he was the one who shouted "go". He'd come back gloating, saying, "I thought you were supposed to be a centre". He was an institution at Saints, part of the woodwork and a quality player too.

I only started two first team games in the 1984–85 season, one at centre, and once at full-back. I came off the bench a couple of times as well. That was a good side which picked up two trophies.

Sean Allen signed for Saints at the same time as me and played in the under-17s with me. He was probably one of the most intelligent players to play for the club. He had 'O' and 'A' levels coming out of his ears. He and Neil Holding used to wear Walsh boots which were the dearest boots you could get, the rest of us had to make do with Puma. They got two pairs, one for training and one for playing in. The week after the lads got these boots we went into training. Neil was wearing the Walsh boots but Sean wasn't, instead wearing his old boots. Kitman Eric Leach asked where his new boots were. Sean replied, "They always rub the first week." I wondered who was wearing them for him. Another time, we were talking about someone who had financial problems and Sean said, "Yeah, he is up to his neck in eyeballs" rather than "up to his eyeballs in debt". Then, when spying a hungry teammate devouring a meal at the club, Sean would announce, "Look at him, he's like a kipper on a tramp". All I could picture was a kipper nibbling a tramp on the floor. All these from a bloke who can speak Russian!

There was another Australian Saints brought over with Mal and Phil called Paul Hamson. He couldn't even get in the 'A' team. He had a great physique, looked belting in training, but just couldn't play.

Saints had signed Australian test star Mal Meninga, who was a quiet bloke who kept himself to himself. He was more into eating chicken than going out drinking. He would have a full chicken for breakfast, earning him the nickname in the dressing room of 'Chicken George'. I'm not sure whether anyone ever said it to his face mind you. He wasn't really a socialiser, certainly not in the same league as some of the players at Saints then. Some of the drinking sessions were unbelievable.

I remember my first proper introduction to drinking with some of the team. I was picked for a match in the Premiership away to Hull KR in May 1984. We went up two days before the game and stayed over. I was in the squad and didn't end up playing. The first night there we had a couple of 'liveners'. I wanted to appear smart in front of everyone so I had bought myself a denim jacket which had a belt on it. It was the worst idea I had ever had. Andy Platt took it off me and Neil Holding threw it on to the ceiling fan. It span round for the rest of the night. I started to get to know all of them then.

Billy Benyon called a meeting at Saints during the Meninga season about the drinking culture among the players. There were a few players missing so Billy said we would wait for them before we got started, but that the meeting was about players' drinking habits starting to get out of control. He said the club had a chance to do something that we hadn't been able to do for ages and have a really good season. We had already won the Lancashire Cup and there was potential for more trophies if we curbed the drinking. Next thing the door opened, three players who were known to like a drink walked in, all wearing Hawaiian shirts, shorts, carrying plastic palm trees and a bottle of rum. Billy Benyon couldn't believe it. One player had his head in his hands. Billy picked up on this and said, "See lads, even this guy's disgusted, aren't you?"

"Yeah," the player replied. "How come you never invited me?"

You could go out for a drink with that particular player in the afternoon, go home for your tea, go back out and he wouldn't have moved from the bar. It didn't affect him. He could get up the next morning and feel great. He's still the same today and hasn't put an inch of fat on.

Paul Doherty's dad used to have a pub in Wigan called The Foundry, it isn't there anymore. That was a hotbed for rugby league players looking for a drink. Paul had been at Saints for a couple of years. We had all been out for a drink round St Helens one night; I got a taxi back to Ashton while Paul went back to his dad's pub in Wigan. At four in the morning, he was still in there drinking and about to go home. They heard a tap on the window, it was another player who had got a taxi all the way there to try and join in. It must have cost him £20. Paul's dad told him he was closing up but he let him in and he probably didn't leave until the next day.

One player never seemed to train, but could run faster than me when he had a cig and a pint. He once had a race against a horse in New Zealand plus Darrell Williams and some other players. I'm almost certain the horse won. Our player came third as he said he wouldn't take the inside track where all the horses had been running.

There was a story that Mal Meninga went into a St Helens nightspot of the time, Cindy's, with a waste paper bin on his head for a laugh. One of the bouncers said, "He shouldn't come in here with that on." The other said, "Have you seen the size of him? You tell him to take it off." Meninga, apparently, entered the club with the bin unchallenged. I'd have been in bed at the time of course. I wouldn't have tried to take the bin off him. I wouldn't have liked to have tried to control him.

We used to go in Cindy's as a group, mainly because there weren't many other options in St Helens at that time. There was another nightclub we went to for Andy Platt's stag do; it was called Francois. It was a little, seedy club. I remember the bouncer at the door really staring at me and rubbing his hands together. I don't know what his problem was, considering that Andy Platt had a solid ball and chain round his leg. I told the rest of the lads and we eventually left to go to Cindy's instead, although it took Andy Platt half an hour to get anywhere with that ball and chain.

We never used to get any bother round town, mainly because we were together as a group. It would have been daft to have picked on one of us when we were standing next to some of our forwards.

There was a Christmas fancy dress do one year. Barrie Ledger went as Spiderman, Steve Peters was Superman and Paul Forber was the Incredible Hulk. Forber looked the part, all green, in ripped shirt and shorts. The party was in Thatto Heath so they took the bus to get there. Some lads on the bus were being rowdy, so Forber made them get off. The passengers couldn't believe their luck that the Incredible Hulk was there to look after them. They ended up coming out of the do at around one in the morning. A foot of snow had fallen. It was too late to get a bus back so they started walking home. They spotted a couple whose car had got stuck in the snow. They couldn't get over the fact that Spiderman, Superman and the Hulk pushed them out of the snow. You couldn't make it up.

I remember early in my Saints career we played at the Watersheddings against Oldham. We got changed at the back of the club and then walked through to the pitch. After the game, you had to walk through the crowd to get back to the dressing room. A pint was thrown over one Saints player so I shouted: "Mine's a bitter". It was a good job one of our backs hadn't been there or he'd have licked it up.

It was the same at Post Office Road when we played Featherstone Rovers. They were having new dressing rooms built and we would have to queue up to go to the toilet. I remember one Saints player, in full kit, in the queue for the gents having a smoke before the game. Another year at Featherstone we were leaving after the game. It was a time of great unrest due to the miners' strike. The Featherstone fans could be hostile at the best of times; some of the players' wives were abused and Saints fans had things thrown at them. It's a tough community. As the coach was leaving the ground, a brick smashed one of our windows. Fortunately, it was by one of the directors. It's not a place I'd have gone unless I'd have played rugby. I don't think I'm ever going to say to the kids: "Right, we're going to Featherstone this weekend, take your hard hat and some steelies."

Mal helped Saints to a couple of trophies with the club picking up the Lancashire Cup and Premiership, but it was back to slim pickings when he left. I didn't get a winners medal for the Lancashire Cup or Premiership wins in the 1984–85 season. I was travelling reserve for the Premiership Final.

Meninga going home obviously left a hole but losing Andy Platt later was the killer blow in my opinion. He ended up being one of the best props in world rugby. If we had kept him alongside the likes of tough, skilful blokes like Forber and Arkwright, we may have achieved the success we all wanted.

Billy Benyon took us on a tour of New Zealand at the end of the 1984–85 season. Bernard Dwyer missed out and still complains about it to this day, I always tell him how good it was and how much he would have enjoyed it.

Before that, the only time I had been abroad was to France with the Great Britain Colts in March the same season. I had to borrow a suitcase from my grandma. When I opened it, it was lined with wallpaper it was so old. I had to take it because I had nothing else, I used to try and leave my kit over it so the lads wouldn't see the brown wallpaper.

By the time the plane to New Zealand had got to Los Angeles, it had run out of beer. Billy started with his strongest team in the first game, but we had a couple of injuries so I got my chance. I did well in the second and third games and I got a good write-up from Ronnie Barker in the *St Helens Star*.

We went to a nightclub in Auckland during the tour. A Maori hooker who was playing for Leigh at the time took us there. It turned out to be a proper gangsters' club. We were all having a drink and noticed a lot of the blokes in there were wearing bandannas. We decided to drink up and move on. We didn't realise but it was about 3 o'clock at this point. Some of the players got taxis. Barrie Ledger, Paul Forber, Sean Allen and I jumped on the back of a bread van. I don't know how we survived the journey. The four of us were just clinging to a piece of string as the van did 60 miles an hour through the streets of Auckland. As we sped along, we were chucking loaves of bread off it. We stopped at one point so we pushed Barrie off and started chucking loaves at him. He was sprinting trying to catch up with us. After about a mile, he caught us up and jumped on, not realising we had arrived back at the hotel and it was time for him to get off. I don't think there was any bread left at this point.

That tour to New Zealand was memorable for lots of reasons, not all on the pitch. One night, we went out and I had put on Tony Burke's shirt. It was Steve Peter's stag do. The night went on and shirts got ripped, I think one of my trainers is still on top of a bar in New Zealand. Somebody said, "What are you doing with Tony's shirt on?" He said, "It better not be mine, that's my wedding shirt". I looked down, the pocket was hanging off and it was in a terrible state. He chased me around the hotel and I am of the firm belief that if he had caught me, he would have killed me. I had to hide all night to let him cool down.

The bar was in Christchurch. One player gave the owner a cheque for £15 and it bounced. The bar owner ended up flying over to Auckland to catch up with him. It must have cost him £90 and I'm not sure he got his £15 back.

We played Waikato who beat us 34-24. They had a big side with plenty of Maoris. Afterwards, they had a big hangi where they cook the food in a hole in the ground. They had beer tents as well. There was one big bloke, who was about 25 stones who went by the nickname 'Handsome'. I think he had given himself the nickname. He came over to me and Shaun Allen and asked if we wanted some coke. Shaun said, "I'll stick with lager thanks." I had to tell Shaun I don't think he was talking about Coca Cola.

Back in England, we were still playing winter rugby and the conditions could be brutal. I remember one Christmas when the weather was terrible. We were supposed to be playing Widnes on New Year's Day, a couple of games had been called off and the forecast wasn't good. As it was New Year's Eve, a few of us went out for a drink in the afternoon thinking the game would be called off. After about four or five pints, I told the others we should go outside and see what the weather was like because if the game was going to go ahead the next day we would have to stop drinking. We went outside, it was below freezing point. Tony Burke stamped around saying "the ground is solid as a rock, there is no chance this game is going to be on". I told one of the players to stop drinking straight away. He asked why and I told him that Tony had just been stamping on a manhole cover. Luckily, the game was eventually called off.

I only played rugby once with a hangover. I met two players on a Friday afternoon in Ashton. We had a few drinks which turned into a few more. I was rough as anything on the Saturday in training and still rough on matchday. I have never been able to handle my ale. We travelled to Hull KR on the Sunday and I still feel sick thinking about it now. In the first five minutes, I took an interception near my own line and went the length of the field to score. I followed this by vomiting behind the posts.

The only other time I played after alcohol was after I had played for Great Britain. We had clinched a 2–1 series win against New Zealand in 1989 on the Saturday and all went out to celebrate. Saints were playing the next day but I didn't think I would be needed. I turned up at the ground - lo and behold I was playing. I scored a try and kicked 10 goals against Barrow so it wasn't too bad. Nobody ever drank the night before a game really.

There was a motorway service station that had an arrangement with Saints where, on the way to away games, we would stop and get all our food for free. We would be on the healthy option of scrambled egg on toast but the directors would load up on bacon and sausages. Seeing that, you couldn't resist it, you'd end up with the full Monty.

Then they used to make us get off the coach a mile before the away ground and walk the rest of the way there. The mile-long walk was to get all the stiffness out of our legs, that or walking all the sausages off. The 20 minute walk was alright; some lads would have a smoke or have a chat. It was better than being stuck on the coach especially if it had been a long trip to Workington.

Now, if you were doing this in Cumbria, it always felt about minus 10. And then we would get into the dressing room and the pegs would be about seven feet high which made us wonder how big the players were. It was a bit daunting for players who weren't used to it.

I remember playing at Whitehaven. Tony Burke and I were on the bench. Tony was coming back from an injury and was dying to get on the field. About half an hour into the game, somebody needed to come off and Tony was given the shout to replace him. He jumped up, forgetting he was sitting in a dugout with a concrete roof. He split his head open, the shout changed to "stitch him up, Paul you will have to go on instead". I don't think Tony felt it, the roof did. I think they needed to use around 100 yards of bandage to cover his head. Tony was a great prop though who would take the ball in all day.

There was a Lancashire Cup semi-final in October 1985 at Central Park against Wigan that was one of the first matches for their giant South African forward Nick du Toit. I played full-back that night. I had been deputising for Phil there while he was back home in Australia. He returned and they played him at centre keeping me at full-back. We got hammered. There were about 18,000 there for this game with a lot of them keen to see du Toit. He got the ball and steamrollered through four of our defenders. It was down to me and him. He looked like a bull on the charge; I was 13 stones with my eyes closed hoping for the best. As he trampled over me, I must have caught his boot lace and somehow brought him down. In the same game their Australian international prop Greg Dowling was playing his second match. It was a night match and all week we had been winding Paul Forber up about Dowling. We said Dowling was going to do him. In the dressing room, Forber was spewing and sweating, muscles and eyes bulging. He said, "They call him the wall. I'm a builder; I've been knocking walls down all my fucking life". From the kick off, the ball went to Forber, who did a little scissor kick and charged straight into Dowling. There was blood and snot everywhere, the crowd winced and groaned. Forber had come off second best. He never heard the last of it. That was the only time it happened to him though. Usually, he was on the other end.

There was one 'A' team game I played with him against Doncaster. They had two old prop forwards who had been about the game for years. Paul went into a tackle and knocked both of them out. He stood over them posing like boxer Chris Eubank. He used to clout me by accident. He and Roy both did as a matter of fact. You'd be minding your own business completing a tackle when one of them would come charging in as second man and would invariably give me a crack.

Saints got rid of Billy Benyon as coach in November 1985 which I felt was a bit unfair because he had won the Lancashire Cup and the Premiership. He was giving the young local lads a chance, including me. The only good thing about him going was that we did not have to compete with him in training. He certainly made the players fit.

Billy Benyon

"When I first met Paul, the first thing I noticed was that he was quite a big lad. He was tall and rangy. He was quiet, a very different character from his dad who I had played against. He had a lot of potential. When he first came to the club, we were more looking at him as a full-back. As he learnt the game at the professional level, he adapted really well in the centre.

Like every other good player, he had his strengths and qualities. He had all the attributes that top players have, he had the lot.

It's difficult to pick out how easy he was to coach because I coached the group rather than individuals. When he first got into the side, he went about his business well and did everything that was asked of him at training. He had his goalkicking too which was another asset. He was a really good all round player.

Like a number of young players that came through the St Helens ranks, he reached the peak of the sport. Even as a 17-year-old, you could see he had a lot of potential."

With Alex Murphy after breaking the club 'points in a game' and 'goals in a game' records in 1986.

3. Alex Murphy in charge

Alex Murphy came in as the new coach and was trumpeted as 'The Messiah' by the local press. A couple of the more experienced players had issues with him. I always got on with Alex; to the point that the lads would say: "He's your dad". He always used to look after me. One year, we had a Christmas party at Joe Pickavance's brother's house. It was a big house with a swimming pool. Scarily, it was free beer so everyone was there. One player pushed the secretary Geoff Sutcliffe in the swimming pool. Geoff had his suit and expensive watch on so wasn't too impressed. The next thing one of the forwards was in, on his back, in just his undies spraying water from his mouth like a whale. A lot later on, that player had drunk a bit too much and went into the part of the house where they were having a disco. He was out of control and upset one of the other players, who smacked him one, knocking three of his teeth out and splitting his lip. The punch broke the offended player's hand. We carried the forward out. He tried coming back in again. I was trying to calm him down. I ended up sitting on his legs with Bernard Dwyer on his chest. Bernard had an expensive shirt on that he had bought from Ken Jeffries. All the buttons were ripped off his shirt and his chest was scratched.

That was it until Alex found out about it. On the Monday, he had us all in for a meeting. He said: "I've got players here, one with no teeth, one with a broken hand and a lad with scratches on him. We've got a big match at the weekend and if anything had happened to him [pointing to me] you'd be on the next boat to Siberia." I got massive stick then, and was called 'Murphy's lad' and so on.

We'd go on training runs and I was far from being a good long distance runner. Even so, Murphy would come in after training and say "best trainer today Paul Loughlin" and give me a free tracksuit. I wanted all this to stop.

Before big games, he would take us to Blackpool. We would stop over for a couple of nights. The first night, we were allowed to have a couple of drinks - you can guess what that turned into. There used to be a pub there called The Gin but that sign made it look like 'gym'. We would tell Murphy we were off to the gym and he would be really pleased with our dedication. One night, we were in there for Paul Doherty's birthday and had a shedful of ale. The next day, we were in training, running all the grog off then going into the sauna and steam room which was great. After that, Murphy announced we all had fish, chips and mushy peas waiting for us. This would be the day before we played Wigan.

In 1985-86 the club signed an Australian goalkicker and centre Ross Conlon. He played for half a season and went back home to resume his career in Australia. I took over as the main goalkicker. Alex Murphy was interviewed on television after a match and said "We don't need to keep bringing these Australians over on big money when we have young, local players like Loughlin. He's had a top game and he's got a kick like a Dobbin." That was it, the nickname stuck among some fans.

Geoff Sutcliffe received a letter of complaint about the interview the Monday after the game and read it to me in his office. A woman had wrote in saying she had been watching the game with her grandchildren and couldn't believe the language coming out of Murphy's mouth describing the young Paul Loughlin on a family show as having "A dick like a Dobbin". Geoff had to write back and tell her she'd heard it wrong.

I'm still the record goals-in-a-game and points-in-a-game record holder at Saints. It came in the 1986−87 season when we played Carlisle in the Lancashire Cup on 14 September at Knowsley Road. It was something I never expected to happen. The previous record was 14 goals held by Geoff Pimblett. There was one game where I kicked 12 and Geoff joked with me after the game that I had nearly beaten his record. During the Carlisle game, I got up to 13 and as I was lining up the next shot at goal, they announced over the tannoy that the kick would "equal the club record". Despite this added pressure, I slotted it over. My next kick, they announced would "break the record" and I missed it from the touchline. Fortunately, I ended up getting to 16 although I missed another four. At one point during the game, Graham Liptrot came up to me and said if I kicked another goal, I would break the record for points in a game too. We ended up winning 112−0.

Barrie Ledger
"Alex Murphy once told Paul he needed new boots because the boots they supplied at Saints weren't the best to be honest. Paul came back and had actually spent £9.99 on the cheapest pair of boots he could find. He kicked all those goals against Carlisle in them! They weren't

exactly a well-known brand; everyone else had been spending £70 on their boots. That was him all over.

He had a fantastic career though and did better than most. I never had to look for him and he never had to look for me, we had that connection where we knew where each other was."

I thought the records may go in 2007 when Saints played Batley in the Challenge Cup. Youngster Ste Tyrer kicked 10 goals in the first half alone. I was listening to it on the radio thinking "if it goes, it goes, it was nice having it". He only got one more in the second half.

After beating Carlisle, we beat Warrington and then played Wigan at Central Park in the Lancashire Cup semi-final and were winning. There was a problem with the floodlights and they went off. When they were switched back on, we ended up losing. There were rumours Wigan did it on purpose. It's one of those things though and I remember the same thing happening at Saints once.

Alex didn't do much of the hands-on training, preferring to leave it to Clive Griffiths. Clive was really good; if it hadn't been for him we would have been on the front training field doing press ups and laps. He brought in lots of different training techniques.

While we trained, Alex would be in the boardroom in his suit while his assistant Dave Chisnall assisted with the training. When we finished, he would hang his suit up, join us in the bath and tell us stories of when he played.

It obviously wasn't full-time training at this time. We would train on a Monday having physio and then do a seven-mile run which I used to hate as I was never a good long-distance runner. We used to set off and go up the big steep hill at Prescot Road. I would always be jogging in the middle of the pack and could never understand that when I finally got back to Saints I would see Lippy and a few others on their way home carrying their bags. There was no way he could have beaten me. I later found out that when they got to the bottom of Prescot Road, they were jumping on a bus to take them part of the way. What finally gave their game away was when Lippy went zooming past me up the hill on someone's bike.

Our trainer, Eric Hughes, found out that some players were cutting corners so he rounded us all up in a minibus and dropped us off at New Golborne roundabout. It was exactly nine miles from Saints ground and it meant there was no way of cutting corners. It was the longest run of my life. Eric Hughes ended up going mad because Alex Murphy picked up Stuart Evans in his car and drove him back to the club. There was no way the 22-stone Evans was doing nine miles.

He was a big signing from rugby union in September 1987, but was too big for rugby league; he was a nice bloke though. You had to laugh at his jokes because he had a 52-inch chest and biceps like an American wrestler. In his first game when he got tackled, he laid the ball off as if he was still playing union; the opposition picked the ball up and scored. But you ran at him at your peril.

On a Tuesday we would do fitness work with huge tyres on the front training pitch at Saints. It was meant to improve our tackling technique, but I never encountered a giant tyre full of air on match day. I just used to close my eyes and hope that the valve wouldn't hit me in the teeth.

Gary Greinke was one of the Australians who came to the club and I thought didn't set the world alight. Kitman Eric Edwards could have beaten him in a race. Nobody had heard of him, I don't know where we were signing some of them from. We do seem to have an obsession with Australia when it comes to rugby league in this country. I remember once there was a backpacker in St Helens and the club wanted to give him a trial just because he was Australian. We did a pre-season run and the lad finished about four miles behind Roy Haggerty and he was one of the worst long-distance runners at the club. We never saw the lad again.

Steve Halliwell had finished top of the try-scoring charts with Leigh and then joined Saints in July 1986. There was a rumour that he hadn't shared his prize money with his Leigh team-mates who weren't too happy about it. As luck would have it, his first game for Saints was against Leigh. He got the ball and got flattened. He only had a short Saints career, and left to join Wakefield the following February.

Dave Tanner was a good clubman and had come from Fylde rugby union in September 1987. His dad would come to watch him in games. Paul Forber used to say his dad would bring his butler with him because Dave was very well spoken, coming from Lytham St Annes. When I was out injured, Dave was doing the goalkicking. You could hear his dad in the stand saying, "One to the left David, two to the right, head down, over it goes" at the top of his voice in a posh accent. We used to take the mick out of him saying, "Your dad's here again with your butler".

We were in Dave Tanner's car in Blackpool once. We got out of the car and were messing about. Les Quirk climbed into the boot and as a joke we shut it on him. He shouted out to us, "Oi, I've got the bloody keys in my pocket". We laughed at first then realised he was serious. The car had a proper boot so we couldn't get at it through the back seat. After about an hour of trying to get into the boot, we went to a police station. A copper came and rescued Les by opening the boot with a coat hanger. When Les had gone in the boot, he had been wearing a tracksuit. When he came out, he was wearing cut-off denim shorts and a t-shirt on plus a change of trainers. His hair had been freshly Brylcreemed too. We asked him what he had been up to and he said it had given him something to do while he was trapped. I don't know how he managed it in the tiny space. He wasn't too happy at the time - but he did see the funny side eventually.

A memorable game in 1987 was when we travelled to Central Park to play Wigan on Boxing Day. We were losing 22–6 at half-time and ended up winning 32–22. Phil Veivers had a brilliant game in the second half. We had done something similar to them the season before, which came up in our half-time team talk – we said we had done it before and could do it again. We were throwing the ball about like Saints always do and everything seemed to come off for us. The pitch was a quagmire as it always seemed to be at Central Park. It was nice beating them, it didn't happen often after that game though.

Paddy Loughlin

"One of the highlights of Paul's career was when Saints beat Wigan 32–22 after trailing 22–6 at half-time. Alex Murphy had been using Paul to take goals from one side of the field and Dave Tanner to take goals from the other, something I didn't agree with. During the game, Tanner was going to take a shot at goal and Paul took the ball off him and kicked it himself. I am glad he did because my argument was if Tanner was ever injured and Paul hadn't kicked from that side of the field for five or six weeks it was going to be harder for him. Anyway, Paul booted it over from the touchline and that ended Murphy's experiment of using two kickers."

The Boxing Day games against Wigan were the highlight of the season. It did mean the players couldn't have a proper drink at Christmas, but we made up for it after the game if we had won. Then there was the build up for our other big game, the New Years Day game against Widnes.

Wigan always had a good side, but then they went full-time and started to build an even better side, with players such as Shaun Edwards, Graeme West, Brian Case and Ian Potter. They ended up signing Joe Lydon, Andy Gregory, Ellery Hanley, Andy Goodway, David Stephenson, Steve Hampson, Kevin and Tony Iro, Andy Platt and many more. They could probably have fielded two top sides. If somebody left, they just replaced him with another international.

The Saints-Wigan rivalry was more about achieving something for your supporters. We would want to win for them because we knew how much it meant to them. A lot of the players from both sides knew each other, especially those involved in the international setup. Even so, there was rivalry and players from both sides would raise their game for the fixture. In 1995, just after I had left to join Bradford, Saints took a bunch of 'A' teamers to Central Park for a first team match, because the club had a Regal Trophy semi-final the next week and another first team match three days later. The young lads played like I had never seen them play before. They lost 58-4, but they did themselves credit – especially the local lads in the side. It did mean a lot to beat Wigan, and not just them, but also Widnes and Warrington in the other local derbies.

However, the toughest games to play in were always against Warrington, especially at Wilderspool. They had players such as Paul Cullen, Les Boyd, Mike Gregory, Kevin Tamati and Bob Jackson. It meant a physical game. I remember one night Graham Liptrot came late into a tackle and smacked Les Boyd. Harry Pinner said to Lippy, "What have you done that for? He'll kill you." Lippy said he was just about to be taken off. Lo and behold, the official on the sidelines was holding up the number 9 for Lippy to be replaced. As he made his way over the official asked him where he was going. Then he looked up and turned the number the right way round, it was number 6 going off. Lippy looked terrified and asked Harry Pinner if in the next scrum he could go loose-forward and Harry take his place in at hooker. Harry just shouted, "Get in the ... scrum." Les Boyd did get his own back. He and Roy Haggerty also had a set-to once and when they were pulled apart, Roy had a cut under his eye. It wasn't very often anyone got the better of Roy.

There are a number of urban legends surrounding Roy Haggerty that circulate not only in the town of St Helens, but the world of rugby league so I thought I'd clarify them. It is true that he was once subbed at Dewsbury in 1986, went in the shower and was unexpectedly brought back into the game with shampoo still in his hair. To make matters worse, it was raining so his hair started frothing up.

A story attributed to Roy about a cash machine is actually about another of our forwards. Basically, cash machines had just been introduced and the player involved wasn't sure how they worked. A friend told him to put your card in the slot then tell it how much he wanted. He inserted his card, leant in and shouted "£10 please".

The story about Roy going on tour to New Zealand and when told there was no bacon at the hotel restaurant, allegedly replying "eight million sheep and you've got no bacon?" is just a joke.

I roomed with Roy on my international debut in France. He had a bag in his room. I asked him what was in it and he told me it was full of Pot Noodles as he wasn't keen on "All that foreign stuff". He had also brought a little portable television over with him, when I asked why he had brought it, he explained, "Well they don't have *Coronation Street* over here."

Another story was when Michael O'Connor and Paul Vautin came to the club; they were both given sponsored cars. Roy was annoyed by this because he was struggling up Prescot Road hill on a pushbike. He went in to see Alex Murphy and asked why, after all his years of service to the club, did he not have a car? Murphy replied simply, "You don't have a licence Roy."

There's a similar story that did the rounds about another local player aggrieved at the perks overseas players were getting. Murphy walked into the dressing room, pointed at one Australian and said, "He's going to need a cortisone injection." The local lad commented: "If he's getting a car, I want one too."

Away from the funny tales, Roy was made of granite and was an honest player. There was one game against Hull KR when Roy was told to get stuck into their international winger. He said he would and did. He got the ball from the kick off and Roy was waiting for him, he smashed him with a forearm - there was nose, blood and teeth everywhere. The next time it was kicked to the winger he just passed it and never went anywhere near Roy again.

31

Roy could also be a skilful player and had been a good centre, but he moved into the second-row. There were no legs on him; he was just all upper body. He was a good player to play off when he let the short ball go - a proper St Helens hero.

Brett Clarke was a classy Australian half-back who joined us in September 1986. He was a good player and played in the Challenge Cup final in 1987. He was quick, skilful and developed a good partnership with Neil Holding, even if his hair did make him look like Barbara Streisand. I met him years later when I went over on the World Club 'holiday' with Bradford in 1997. [2] He's not changed.

We went to the Stones Bitter Player of the Year awards in 1987 at Lord Daresbury's where I was awarded Young Player of the Year and also an award for being the top goalkicker that year. I was given a cheque with £5 for each goal I had kicked that year. We had a good drink at the hotel, in fact we were still behind the bar pulling ourselves pints at six in the morning. The barman had given up and gone to bed hours before saying he was going to leave us to it. There were about 20 people there serving themselves in the end.

We decided it would be a good idea to go Sutton Manor Colliery where Chris Arkwright worked and have our breakfast there. So, we went down to the pit, still in our tuxedos from the night before, with a bottle of sherry. We had scrambled eggs in the miners' canteen. The lads coming up after their shift must have wondered what was going on; mind you they were greeting Arkie as if it was a regular occurrence. We even had miners' helmets on. After that, we went to Barrie Ledger's mum's pub and carried on. There was a training session at Saints the next day and I believe only two players turned up. That was my first real introduction of what it was like to be a 1980s Saints player, a proper one. You know you've made it when you're having scrambled eggs on toast in Sutton Manor Colliery.

Paul Forber ('Buffer') was a player I felt was incredibly underrated, he was fast; he could kick goals, pass both ways, sidestep and knew how to handle himself too. I used to love playing outside him because he would draw two players into the tackle and put me into space with a little inside pass. He never seemed to get international recognition,

---

[2] In 1997, all the European and Australasian Super League teams participated in the World Club Challenge. The European teams were generally outclassed and it was felt that some of the players saw the trip down under as a time for relaxation.

possibly down to the amount of time he spent as a substitute at Saints. I think he deserved better. He was sick before every single game. His arms were always bulging and his head band was on tight.

He liked a bet on the horses. When Alex Murphy was coach he used to let Forber out of training to put his bets on for the greyhounds. There was a cup tie against Leeds at Headingley one year; we were at the ground waiting to go on the coach. We asked where Forber and Lippy were, Murphy told us they were in the betting shop at the side of the Black Bull pub and wouldn't be long. Forber and Lippy ended up buying a greyhound between them; I don't think it won much. After Paul's playing career, he used his money wisely, he had a chip shop, a sunbed shop, was a builder and so on. He passed me one day in a massive jeep, he told me how much it had cost and asked me what I was driving. I certainly didn't have a massive jeep.

Phil Veivers was a consistent performer throughout his time at Saints and had a long career at the club. Away from the club, Phil, John Harrison and I would train together. We would socialise together every Thursday. Then it became every weekend. It ended up where I bought a house near Phil in Garswood. This was partly so I could get a lift. When I was about 23, I was prosecuted for drinking and driving. It was a big mistake and I've never done it since. I had just got a brand new Peugeot 405 from Broughton's Garage as a sponsored car from the club. Two weeks later, I got caught drinking and driving.

Phil took me to the Wigan Magistrates Court. I explained he needed to go with me because he would be the one driving back. I drove the car on the way there because I knew it would be a while before I would be behind a wheel again.

The judge told me I was a role model for young people. I apologised for my behaviour, told him I was ashamed of myself and would never do it again. The judge said: "It's people like him" pointing at Phil. Now Phil had obviously been day dreaming because he stood up immediately. The judge said: "There's no need to stand up Mr Veivers, please sit down." He then continued: "It's people like him who will have to drive you around." Phil agreed, "Yeah, yeah, that's right" and he clearly didn't have a clue what the judge had been saying.

I got an 18-month ban from driving. I had been well over the limit, and as I looked out of the window, I thought I could still see a chorus line of can can girls dancing. Phil took my keys and as we left the court, he said: "I've got some news for you. This car is now mine. The club rang me up yesterday but I didn't want to tell you before you went to court." He had my brand new car. Fair play to Phil, he picked me up for training and work. I don't forget support like that. When my ban was up, my next sponsored car was not as nice.

In January 1988 we beat Leeds in the John Player Special Trophy Final at Central Park, I scored two tries and three goals. However, Neil Holding got all the headlines with his winning drop-goal in a 15–14 victory. He was even on the front page of a special St Helens edition of the *Sunday Mirror*. He still tells me today about how he won that cup for Saints. I think Andy Platt made 44 tackles that day; I would have struggled making that in a season. Roy Powell, the Leeds forward, made an incredible 50 tackles. We were underdogs that day because they had some quality international players including Garry Schofield, Peter Jackson and David Creasser. It was another quagmire of a pitch at Wigan. I remember taking a pass from Neil and heading for the line, I didn't even know if I had made it over the line but I just jumped up and the referee gave it. In the second half, I took a pass from Paul Forber in my own half, went through and rounded the Leeds full-back to score.

Going up the steps for that John Player Special Trophy was magic, especially after scoring most of our points. I thought that would have been the launchpad for bigger and better things for Saints. We were still a few players short, but I thought this could have been the start of something big for us. Shane Cooper and Neil Holding were good at half-back and Andy Platt was still at the club. It wasn't the same as winning at Wembley, but it was a good feeling nonetheless.

It was a good night out afterwards too because all the Saints lads used to stick together back then. We would have a drink and disco at Saints after games, with George Mann as one of the ringleaders and Paul Forber taking over the microphone.

There were a lot of top players linked with transfers to Saints in the late 1980s and early 1990s; such as Jonathan Davies, David Campese and so on. They never materialised. It annoyed the supporters, but for players, if their position under threat, they would hope it wasn't true. If the club signed top players, they would be in the team and somebody would have to make way for them. I remember Brendan Hill coming training with us one Saturday morning. He failed a medical apparently and signed for Halifax instead. Later on, he tore us apart in the 1989 John Player Special Trophy semi-final. The best signing we ever made while I was at the club was Shane Cooper; he had a massive long-term impact. There were other Kiwis, including Mark Elia, George Mann and Tea Ropati, but Cooper was the best one for me. He was a good player and if it wasn't for his presence in some seasons, we would have really struggled because he was a good leader.

Shane Cooper

"There is not much I need to say about a person who has represented his country more than a dozen times, been on two tours 'down under' and been picked by his Great Britain team mates as 'Most Valuable Tourist' on one of those occasions. His humour is second-to-none and I don't think I have ever seen the big lad from Ashton without a smile on his face. Even during his bad injury run he was giving the lads encouragement."
(From The Paul Loughlin Souvenir Testimonial Brochure)

We played Widnes in the 1988 Premiership Final at Old Trafford. We had a few players missing and so fielded a depleted team with some players out of position. I played full-back that day; it was shortly before the Australian tour so I was desperately hoping I wouldn't get injured in the game. Widnes were at full strength. We started off well but they tore us to shreds with Kurt Sorenson picking up the Harry Sunderland award for man-of-the-match. They ran riot. I remember everyone was talking about Martin Offiah and his pace at the time and I was praying I wouldn't end up one-on-one with him. But it ended up being Darren Wright who did me. He broke down the wing and I couldn't lay a finger on him. I tried to dive to get him in the corner but it was too late. They were a quality side though who could match Wigan at that time.

There was talk after the 1988 tour of me going to Wigan. I went to see the Saints chairman, Joe Pickavance, and told him what I had heard. He said there was no way I was leaving so I asked if my money could be put up. It did go up, but not by much. I would have made a lot more at Wigan. They needed a goalkicker at the time because David Stephenson was leaving. I could have ended up with lots of winners' medals at Wigan and possibly wouldn't have to work today. This was at the same time as Andy Platt leaving Saints. I didn't really want to play for Wigan though being a Saints lad.

The 1988 John Player Trophy Final

Touching down under the posts. (Courtesy *St Helens Reporter*)

Celebrating a narrow victory. (Courtesy *St Helens Reporter*)

To be honest the contractual setup at Saints is the reason I believe that Andy Platt left the club. When he returned from the 1988 Australian tour, I think Saints only offered him around £7,000 per year. Wigan were offering him full-time money, about £30,000 per year. The fans called him Judas, the same as they later did with Gary Connolly. They've got to put themselves in the player's position though. If you are a plasterer, for example, and a plastering firm from Wigan offers you a massive pay increase you are going to take it.

I believe that's where Saints fell short with the local lads. They exploited the fact that we were all keen to play for the side and offered the bigger money to Australian players, the majority of whom weren't that good. They were on four times as much money as the rest of us and it caused problems. There were local lads like Paul Forber, Paul Round and Roy Haggerty in the pack working their hearts out - big, hard tough forwards. They then signed an Australian forward who had only won one test cap and was paid loads more than them.

There was also talk of me going to Widnes. Their coach Doug Laughton had picked me for Lancashire. When I was on tour with Great Britain I would hang out with the Widnes lads including the Hulme brothers, Andy Currier and Darren Wright. They were all good lads. I had played rugby union at West Park School with Paul Hulme. There was nothing concrete behind the talk, just an enquiry.

As part of the pre-match entertainment for the Widnes versus Canberra World Club Challenge in 1989, I took part in a goalkicking contest for the leading goalkickers. There was me, Lee Crooks, Mark Aston and John Woods. We had to take shots at goal from kicking tees placed on different parts on the pitch. If you missed, you were out. It came down to me and Lee Crooks. We kept going further and further back until we ended up on the halfway line. Lee missed his kick. I remember Keith Macklin saying over the tannoy: "Paul's got this kick for £1,000." Talk about pressure! Behind him was Neil Holding jumping up and down like a monkey in a hot bath because the money would be going into the Saints players' kitty. I got a nice decanter from my success. It was one of those days I just didn't miss a shot.

South Sydney had also been interested in me, but Saints knocked it back. I had been going through some injury problems at the time. I also held talks with Gold Coast who rang me at home. Of course, there were no agents then, so it was all direct talks. They made me a good contract offer including an apartment near the beach; it was fantastic.

I went to Saints to discuss it but they said "no". I'd have loved living and playing over there. I think their hard pitches would have suited me. Better there than slogging it out in the mud and rain.

Eric Ashton

"Paul is St Helens through and through and was prepared to throw in his lot with his home town team rather than go elsewhere. He is a great goalkicker and most important of all – a winger's centre! There are many good centres around, but only a select few are in that particular category."

David Howes

"God made a special mould for 'Lockers'! Not only is he built in the classic centre style of height and elegance, reminiscent of a Gasnier or Ashton, but he is also an ace goalkicker. The mould, however, extends to his personality, so laid back that he is rugby league's version of the Tower of Pisa."

(Both from The Paul Loughlin Souvenir Testimonial Brochure)

Saints signed Australian test players Michael O'Connor and Paul Vautin for the 1988–89 season. I know Michael O'Connor has been very critical of the training he did while at Saints. He would have liked to have seen more moves. Alex Murphy thought that rugby was a simple game and he didn't want to complicate things, it was a case of running hard and tackling hard. He felt moves just confused players. I think rugby today is going back to how it was then; you don't see moves from the scrum these days. Paul Vautin did well at Saints but I don't think O'Connor really enjoyed the weather over here. He's probably right that we were a little basic in our approach at the time though.

Alex even offered a trial to Wimbledon footballer Vinny Jones. Jones was a centre of attention at the time, having been photographed grabbing Paul Gascoigne's testicles and being known as a hard man on the pitch. I don't know if he would have survived long in rugby. He would have been a target for sure. His career would have been over in five minutes. Gary Mason, the boxer, had a trial with London Crusaders, but if it's not in you to be a rugby player, you won't get very far. I think the Vinny Jones episode was just a publicity stunt.

The Wimbledon football team, the 'Crazy Gang' used to listen to a tape in the dressing room to get them wound up before games, Wigan brought it into rugby league by trying listening to motivational tapes. At Saints, we used to listen to *Eye of the Tiger*, it might have got the forwards going but certainly not laid back Paul.

At the end of one season, we all went to the Isle of Man as a group. We got on the plane at 9.00am and started drinking. There were about 40 of us because the 'A' team came with us as well. They were all nutters. As soon as the plane was ready for take-off one player let off a stink bomb. We couldn't get there fast enough.

We arrived and got on a coach to take us to the hotel. There was a little old man sat at the front on the mike giving us a guided tour. We were all laughing and heckling him saying he looked like he was off the Benny Hill show. He told us we were about to go over the Fairy Bridge and that if we didn't say "hello fairies" then we would have bad luck for the rest of the trip. As we went over the bridge all you could hear was deep voices trying to say "hello fairies" as quietly as possible.

It was a big hotel, with five floors, I was sharing with Shane Cooper, Mike Riley, Les and my mate Deano who had joined us. We were on the top floor and I heard a bang on our window. We were about 40 feet up and as I got to the window, I was greeted by a naked Saints player who had shimmied his way round the outside of the hotel. He said, "Any chance of letting me in, it's getting a bit cold up here."

One of this player's party tricks was to turn up at various occasions with little clothing on. The pick of these was at the Isle of Man when he came down to the hotel bar naked save for a blow up doll tied around his waist. He ordered a pint then said: "Just a short for the lady". He put the short in the doll's hand then put it to his mouth to drink it. It ended up that the doll was banging into people only for the player to say: "Excuse the lady, she's no manners". None of us ever questioned this, we just let him get on with it.

Frankie Barrow and Buffer had organised the trip, we all pooled our money on a big bet on a horse race and, as luck would have it, it came in for us. We won a grand for our kitty.

The owner of the hotel had a big tropical fish tank in reception. They were his pride and joy, he told us he didn't mind if we smashed up the hotel as long as we didn't touch his fish. When we left, the tank was still there but inside it was a little bridge, a little flower, some bubbles coming up and that was it... We used the betting money we had won to pay for the damage we had done to the hotel and to buy some new tropical fish. I didn't go back to the Isle of Man for years.

I did go back to the Isle of Man for a stag party with a pal from the Old Road Labour Club. I had been going there for years, it's a good club and I was mates with a lot of the lads who went there. On our next to last day, we were playing pool in a backstreet pub. One of the lads was well known for the size of his wedding tackle. He went into the gents, came back with not a stitch on and started playing pool using his old lad as a cue. All the lads were laughing and cheering, the landlord wasn't impressed and told him to put his clothes back on because there were two old ladies sitting at the other end of the pub. He apologised and went to go and get his clothes. One of the old ladies shouted, "Hey, hang on, you've still got two shots". The Isle of Man looks nice on the adverts but I've seen the real side of it.

During my testimonial year, 1993–94, we decided to go and call in at a pub in St Helens which one of our players was running at the time. His customers were holding blokes down and shaving all their hair off with dubbers. There were grown men with bald heads, sat with their wives crying in the corner of the pub. The player told me, "Don't come in or you'll end up bald like these". I had my wedge at the time and couldn't lose that.

Once I went in there and there was a bloke nailed to the back door by his ear. Another time, there was someone trying to nail the skin on their testicles to the pool table in an attempt to get a free pint. They were all crazy. They had a beach party in there once. There was sand all over the pub, everyone was wearing Hawaiian shirts and there was plastic palm trees scattered around. Two old men were offered free pints if they did two laps of the pool table and bar with their pants and underpants around their ankles. They then had to bend over and take a whack on their behind without making a noise. All this for a beer. I had a very quick pint and left quickly. Very quickly.

We played at Barrow in a testimonial match for Lippy. That night, we went to a club and the player who had been naked outside our hotel window in the Isle of Man did the s-s-s-slither. One moment, he had all his clothes on. The next, he was naked and slithering across the stage like the advert 'slither'. Earlier that night, we had been in another club and Buffer had taken the mike off the singer giving a

40

rendition of *10 guitars* and sang it himself after saying "You don't sing it like that cock". Everybody was up dancing while Forber sang.

One player who was always lively was Chris Arkwright. He was a great player and if it hadn't been for injury, I think he would have captained Great Britain. He was very tough and skilful. His knee problem may have ended his career but it certainly never changed his attitude towards life.

Back to the rugby, I was surprised when Alex Murphy left Saints. I really liked him and had played some of my best rugby under him. He didn't do a lot of actual coaching, but his knowledge of the game was second to none. He was a good man manager. Some might disagree with me on that point, but I liked him. He worked at St Helens Glass and knew everyone. If players got injured, he would look after them. He would make sure they got a few bob and even take them for a day out. He took Jon Neill and Arkie for a day out to Blackpool once when they were injured with bad knees. He dropped them off, gave them a few quid for something to eat and a drink then went off on some business before picking them up to take them home. Some people never saw that side of him, but he was a nice bloke.

I was gutted when he left because I was playing really well. I know Billy Benyon gave my first starts, but Alex give me a consistent run. He backed me to the hilt and looked after me which I will never forget. As a man manager and a bloke, he was great.

We won the John Player Special Trophy with him in 1988 and he got us to Wembley in 1987 and 1989. We were runners up in the league as well in 1987–88. He did upset a few people though. He would shout and swear at the players at half-time. The most memorable instance of this was when I was out injured with a broken arm. I had been sitting on the bench watching the game in a big coat which covered my cast. I joined the rest of the lads in the dressing room at the interval. At the end of the rollocking Murphy glared at me and screamed: "And you, start running your weight!" I hadn't played for four weeks.

He always used to get on Neil Holding's back, possibly because Neil played in the position Alex was famous for. There was a game where I missed three kicks against Warrington. Alex was going mad shouting at Neil, "Why has he missed those kicks" as if it was Neil's fault. That was what Alex was like. However, I was going through a good patch of

41

my career at the time so I would have been happy no matter who the coach was.

Alex Murphy

"I've always thought Paul is a very, very nice lad. I feel he was always underrated and underestimated as a player. He was a very good, quality player. With him being a bit shy and a bit quiet, some people didn't think he would be able to hack it. He was an excellent player though, a good goalkicker and I would always have him in my side. He could win you games as he was a good footballer with a good pair of hands. He could tackle, yet he wasn't as quick as he would have liked to have been but having said that, he was a good wingman's centre. He could both make and stop tries.

When I took over at Saints, I saw the potential in Paul. There are coaches these days who will have good quality kids in their 'A' teams and won't give them a game. I watched him train, he trained very hard and I thought 'I'm going to give this kid a go'. He made a few mistakes at first which we worked to correct. He was always a lad who listened and he went from strength to strength. I think he is the most underrated player St Helens have ever had but I rated him. He would always be in the selection for my side. He could play in a number of positions too. As a kid he was a little bit concerned to hold his place in a very good St Helens side, which gives you an insight into him.

He was great to have in the dressing room too. Put it this way, I wish I could have 17 like him every week. He was well respected, he got on with all the lads, I don't think anybody ever had a bad word to say about him. He was very likeable."

4. Mike McClennan arrives

Kiwi Mike McClennan took over when Murphy left in January 1990. He was good for some players and not for others. I had most of my injuries while McClennan was at the club. I never had a decent run. When I returned from one of my broken arms, Mike had brought Jarrod McCracken into the side. McCracken got a bit of stick once in the piano bar of 'Crystals' nightclub. This lad was giving him stick and McCracken warned him to keep away. The lad wouldn't listen and kept on at him, Jarrod said he wouldn't tell him again and that he needed to go away. He came over again, Jarrod hit him once and the lad's mates had to carry him out. Fortunately, that was a one off. Jarrod McCracken could have knocked anybody out. It's silly to pick on rugby lads because they are strong and fit as anything.

Paddy Loughlin
"When Mike McClennan came to the club, he tried to change Paul's kicking style. But he had been kicking goals from the touchline since 8 years of age."

However, for some players Mike's coaching methods were good. He gave Bernard Dwyer a regular position at hooker and as a result Bernard never looked back. He developed Jon Neill and John Harrison. Shane Cooper had brought McClennan to the club - he had known him in New Zealand. I thought he was a bit strange. The long words he used, some players just couldn't understand half the time.

One time Mike did help me was when I got sent off against Leigh in March 1990. I had lined up Johnny Kerr in a ball-and-all tackle. As I tackled him, Paul Forber came in with a forearm smash to the top of his head. Johnny went down. The ref said: "Come here Paul". Buffer walked over to him, but the ref sent him away and asked for me. He sent me off.

I had just been selected for the Great Britain tour to Australia and at this time the RFL were handing out six and eight match bans for high tackles so I was worried. Mike went to the disciplinary hearing in Leeds with me. They had a big screen where it showed frame-by-frame what happened in the tackle. I did catch Johnny high, but it was Paul's challenge that did the damage. I got 'sending-off sufficient' thanks to Mike. He asked me to stand up and then fished a bible out of his bag. He put it on the table and said, "Put your hand on the Holy Bible Paul and swear to them that you're not a dirty player." The guys running the disciplinary hearing said, "Whoah, we don't need this". It was the first time they had ever seen anything like it, but it worked.

Mike brought a new move into the game with the very tall John Harrison heading the ball over the line for George Mann to score. Before the game, McClennan had asked the referee whether there was anything in the rule book about heading the ball and he confirmed there wasn't. After that game they banned the move. He had other ideas. Another was that if we were playing Wigan, right at the beginning of the game he would instruct Kevin Ward to start a scuffle. Then George Mann or Jon Neill would smack one of their prop forwards to try and knock him out of the game. His theory was that nobody would get sent off in the first minute of a match.

He also gave the players sachets of Peking Royal Jelly. He reckoned it was for our stamina, but it was also meant to be good for sexual performance. I think six players' wives soon became pregnant.

He was a very deep guy, always thinking about what he was going to say. There was a fans' question and answer session at Greenalls club in St Helens. It was Shane Cooper, Phil Veivers, Mike and me being questioned. The first question went to Mike and he was still responding to it after an hour. I was relieved because it meant I didn't have to say anything. He would go in-depth about everything. He used to have a drink with the lads though. He also got the best out of Kevin Ward and Paul Bishop. He was very tactically astute when it came to picking the weaknesses of other teams.

In training, after the first part of the session McClennan would disappear leaving Stan Wall in charge. We didn't always listen to Stan and ended up pushing each other round the field inside the tyres. Stan wouldn't say anything to us, but maybe used to report back to the powers-that-be.

There was a game against Warrington at Knowsley Road and it was a real stormy night. We had run out and part of the stand fell off and nearly hit Warrington winger Gary Mercer - the match was immediately called off. It could have been me on that side if the toss for ends had gone the other way.

In 1990, we played Wigan in the Challenge Cup semi-final at Old Trafford. In the changing rooms before the game, Mike McClennan had given us all an envelope which he told us not to open until just before we went out onto the field. We did our warm-up then were ready for our last-minute instructions. He told us to open our envelopes. All it had on it was the number and name of the player you were marking that day. Mine was Iro 3. McClennan said "That's all I want you to do today. If you can come in and say you have done better than him that's all I ask of you." I think every Saints player did that on that day.

The try Les Quirk scored that day was sensational; if it had been scored by a more celebrated name like van Vollenhoven it would never be forgotten. There are not many people who get the ball in their own half, go round Joe Lydon, hand him off, then go in-and-out to get past Steve Hampson, - that's two internationals - and then score.

With 90 seconds remaining, the game was level. Ellery Hanley sent Andy Goodway in for the winner off what we thought was a clearly forward pass and our dreams were shattered once again. As well as a fantastic Les Quirk try, Gary Connolly had pulled off a sensational cover tackle on Joe Lydon. Everybody stood up for that game and we were robbed by a bad decision. If we had played anyone but Wigan that day, we'd have put 50 on them. We were playing a test team every time against Wigan. We were so deflated after the game because we knew if we had beaten them, we would probably have won at Wembley. That could have been a turning point for the club. It just wasn't to be – again.

Martin Dermott had one of the best games I've seen him play for Wigan at hooker that day. He and Andy Platt were tackling everybody. And for us George Mann was outstanding. He was also the best singer we've ever had at the club. He had all the soul classics, him and Buffer would take it in turns to sing after a game on a Sunday. The crowd loved him. He liked a drink and a smoke. He was a good lad. When he first came to the club, he was one of the best players in the league. Perhaps his best game was that semi-final against Wigan. Despite suffering from a cut head, he took the Wigan pack to bits that day. After the game Andy Platt commented on how tough he was and for someone of that stature to say something like that means a lot.

I believe that Saints didn't offer George as much as he wanted in terms of his contract and he ended up going to Leeds. He didn't seem to do as well there.

Tea Ropati was another good Kiwi player, someone who was quiet and looked after himself on the weights. When he left Saints, he went to Auckland Warriors and played well for them. That shows what kind of quality he had. When I look back at some of the players we had at Saints, I wonder why we didn't achieve a bit more.

I had a brilliant relationship with Les Quirk. Barrie Ledger had helped me a lot and I learnt from him. When he left Les was his replacement. We had a tremendous partnership; sometimes I would hit a gap and not have to look to send him a pass because I knew exactly where he would be. 'The Cumbrian Express' they used to call him. We really got on and would socialise together away from Saints. I would go to the middle of nowhere in Ulverston, Cumbria where he lived. That was some journey for him to get to Saints.

He scored some amazing tries. There was the last-minute try he scored against Hull to win a game at Knowsley Road. I got the ball near our line, Paul Eastwood came in quickly and I slipped Les a little pass. He went the length of the field. Again, if we hadn't been a struggling side at the time, people would still be talking about what an amazing try it was. Playing alongside me, Les scored 53 tries in 79 matches, some strike record.

It was the same with Barrie Ledger. He went the full length to clinch a game against Warrington at Knowsley Road off a little flick pass from me. This was while Des Drummond was coming to knock my ribs through the other side of my chest. Trying to get my winger away and my goalkicking were my big strengths. Going back to the flick pass, it does make me laugh when people refer to it as 'the Gidley flick' after the recent Saints star. Did he do it before Mal Meninga and Gene Miles?

I was always fortunate to have very fast wingers outside me at Saints such as Ledger, Quirk, Kevin McCormack, Alan Hunte and Anthony Sullivan. It just shows that Saints were fortunate not to have me on the wing.

I had played against Kevin Ward and his other Castleford prop Keith 'Beefy' England many times and they were two big props opponents didn't want to run into. Mike McClennan came to me in training one day and asked me my opinion of Wardy. I had been on tour with him and had roomed with him. He had played in Australia for Manly. He would have the television on in our room watching some Australian comedy programme and be roaring with laughter. I didn't find it funny, but he would look at me after each joke and I would have to do a fake laugh so I didn't upset him.

46

Saints signed Wardy in July 1990 and then Paul Bishop joined us from Warrington in November that year. Wardy was a crowd favourite at Saints and did some good work for the club. He always used to call me 'Tom' for some reason. I actually called my son Tom just in case he ever meets him and I can tell Wardy I named him after me. He would always nip into the off licence that used to be near Saints for some cans for his journey home.

Paul Bishop was a good signing for the club. I had played in the Great Britain Colts with him. He was like a breath of fresh air to the club. It had been horrible playing against him; he was only little but managed to wind everybody up. He had played for Warrington. A player would play-the-ball and he would challenge him and then keep out of their way. He and Wardy formed the perfect small man-big man partnership on the field. My dad did the same thing with Paul's uncle, Alan Bishop. Paul was a good goalkicker too.

We finally managed to overcome Wigan in the 1991 Lancashire Cup semi-final which, unfortunately, I missed due to injury. We beat Rochdale in the final to lift the trophy and it was tough to miss out on that success.

We played Wigan in the Charity Shield at Gateshead in 1992; unfortunately I had a broken arm at the time. The night before the game, the Saints players were all in a nightclub in Newcastle. We hammered Wigan 17–0 and that was a miracle because most of the players were still feeling the effects of the night before. I'm certain some of our players still had kebab stains on their hands and faces.

The club had been looking for new talent to take the side forward. I remember Saints played Oldham. They had a young forward who had a stormer against us. His name was Chris Joynt. The club made a move to sign him and a lot of people were asking "what are we signing him for?" He certainly proved those doubters wrong. He joined the club in September 1992, was a quality signing and a good professional, one of the best Saints have had. The amount of trophies he won and the way he played speaks for itself. For him to be selected to play front-row against the Australians when he usually played as a back-rower shows the esteem and respect in which he was held. He was a great captain too.

We played Wigan in the 1992 Premiership Final at Old Trafford. We started off quite well and I scored two tries. I always seemed to score in finals for some reason, and test matches. Maybe I used to save my tries for television and *Grandstand*. However, Gene Miles dumped Gary Connolly in a big tackle and Wigan ran away with the game. They hammered us in the second half and won 48–16. They turned it on and we couldn't hold them.

They could have fielded two teams at that stage. Even their young players were on more money than the international players at Saints, with the exception of our overseas players who were always looked after. Some of our lads would be doing shift work then training, while Wigan were full-time professionals. It was disheartening. There was a difference in fitness, size and strength. To have a chance against them we would have to be having a very good day and they would have to be slightly off. Those Saints versus Wigan games seemed to bring the best out of us though.

We did get a little jealous, thinking why couldn't a club like Saints get some backers and do the same as Wigan. There was money in the Wigan club at the time with four millionaires on the board, and they improved the club and the team. By contrast, Saints had local business men and professionals. I think there was only Joe Pickavance who had any financial clout. Back then, it seemed that if someone could put a few pounds into the club, they became a director. The directors got a blazer; it took the players 12 games to get one. It was difficult to accept a telling off from someone who owned a pie shop. I thought that most of them did not know much about rugby league. Joe Seddon and Joe Pickavance were always well respected though.

Gary Connolly was a quality player. Probably Saints' biggest mistakes ever were getting rid of Gary and Andy Platt to Wigan at different times. Considering the money they were willing to give to overseas players, I could never work out why two home-grown stars were allowed to leave, especially to our biggest rivals. Talent like that doesn't come round so often. Maybe it's because Gary was a St Helens lad and they thought he'd stay and just play for his club blazer and have his name in the local paper. I went on tour with Gary in 1992 and I was first-choice centre. I got injured; Gary got the jersey and never looked back. He did some off-season training with Alan Hunte and they came back like greyhounds. Gary ended up as a Wigan legend. He enjoyed life off the pitch, but it never seemed to affect his performances. He was one of the hardest players to try and get past.

I had been delighted when Tommy Frodsham left Swinton to join Saints in August 1989. He was probably one of the most skilful half-backs I ever played with. He had brilliant hands, could pass both ways and would pick me out from 20 yards to put me through a gap. He had a lethal sidestep too. If he'd have signed earlier in his career for Saints, I think he'd have been a top international player. He didn't get noticed at Swinton. An incident at the club with Mike McClennan ended his Saints career, and he returned to Swinton in February 1991.

Tommy Frodsham

"I knew of Paul, but I didn't know him personally until I signed for Saints. The first thing that struck me upon meeting him was how laid back he was. He was very welcoming to me, he's a St Helens born lad so he was one of the first people with whom I got on well. He was an established international and took me under his wing a bit. He had a lot of respect for me which I didn't expect.

He is a freak of nature, he shouldn't have been as good as he was because he didn't seem to worry about anything. He never let anything affect him and I never saw him under pressure. He must have felt it at times but he had a good way of not showing it.

Although I had played in the First Division before with Swinton, I had never played alongside players of the calibre of Paul Loughlin. He was dream to play with. His timing was impeccable.

He's the funniest guy you'll ever meet, I was speaking to someone who works with him the other day. All you have to do is say Paul's name to someone who knows him and they will start laughing. He should be on television. One of his and Les Quirk's tricks was to bring mice into training and hide them in lads' kit bags. This happened to me one night resulting in me and my wife chasing a mouse all round our house trying to catch it. I never told Paul about this though because I didn't want to give him the satisfaction.

I had the opportunity to sign for Wigan before going to Saints, I would have been cover for Edwards and Gregory, but the deal fell through when I was injured and I don't regret it for a minute. I'd rather have played for Saints and not missed out on representing my home town club and all the great memories I have. I'd have signed for Saints for nothing. To have the friends I have got from there like Paul and the memories that I have are wonderful. Lockers made life easy for me at the club and it's great getting together with some of those lads these days. They're legends to me.

I am looking forward to reading this book because when we get together Paul will be halfway through a story, stop then tell us: 'You'll have to get my book'."

I was coming back from my broken arm and played in the 'A' team to build up my fitness. We played in the 'A' team cup quarter-final against Wigan. Paul Forber was playing too. Frankie Barrow was coach and when we went in at half-time 10 points down he wasn't best pleased. He started shouting at us that with the team we had out we should be winning. He got hold of the stats and said to Buffer: "Forber, you've only made four tackles, for a second-rower that's just not good enough". Forber just replied: "I'm not being funny Frank, but look at the size of me, who's going to run at me?" Frank said, "I suppose so." Frank then turned his attention to half-back John McAtee and said, "You've only made two tackles." Quick as a flash, McAtee replied, "I've been defending at the side of Buffer." McAtee could have been a good player but I thought he became over-confident.

On 27 December 1992 we played Wigan in what became known as the 'Coors' game. As a one-off, we wore the Coors brewery logo on the front of our shirts against Wigan at Saints. The team Wigan had then was incredible: Offiah, Bell, Platt, Edwards, Betts, Clarke and so on. Botica scored first and converted from the touchline, there was a feeling all round the ground of 'here we go again'. They never scored again. We destroyed them 41−6, it's a shame we never played in those shirts again. Maybe it was the six cans we each had before the game. The game is talked about by Saints supporters to this day with people reciting bits of Sky's commentary from the match:
"Sonny Nickle, running like a man possessed."
"He hits the wall, who cares, the thumb goes to it."
"And why not, around about Christmas time."
"Roll out the barrel cos here comes the Cooper."

Everything just came off that day; even I didn't get any stick. When Saints play like that, free-flowing rugby using Tea Ropati and Alan Hunte who were like racehorses, there was no stopping us. Nobody could have touched us that day. I wish there had been more like it.

Earlier that season, we'd lost to Wigan in the Lancashire Cup Final 5−4 at Knowsley Road, a game I missed due to a broken arm and we only lost the league to them on points difference. We played Wigan in the game that would ultimately decide the title at Central Park. We drew 8–8 and I missed a couple of kicks from the touchline. It didn't seem to matter that Frano Botica was missing kicks that day; I got all the blame for us not winning. It was a day when we matched the great Wigan side. It was also the day a horrific leg injury put paid to Kevin Ward's career. It's the saddest thing I've ever seen on a rugby pitch. All the team went to see him in the hospital and you could tell he wasn't going to be the same man again. We blame that game for losing the league but that same season we had lost at Leigh who had struggled all year. When we drew 8–8 with Wigan, 'Ducky' O'Donnell stopped a drop-goal by touching the ball as it was in the air. As his name was Gus O'Donnell, they called it 'the hand of G-O-D'.

Ducky was buzzing over all the attention. When we worked on the ground, Neil Holding would often go into the press box and ring people up. He decided he would get Ducky and pretended to be Peter Wilson from the *Daily Star*. He rang up Ducky and asked if he could have an interview about the 'Hand of G-O-D' incident. Ducky said no problem and chatted away for 15 minutes. Neil finished the interview by saying, "We normally send the fee for interviews to the players' fund at the club to be shared out among the team or if you like, we can send you the cheque for £3,000 directly to your house." Ducky asked for it to be sent to his house and he could sort it out with the lads later.

We trained the next day; someone asked if anyone had received a phone call from Peter Wilson. Ducky stayed quiet. Someone else said, "He rang me but he wanted to get hold of Ducky." Ducky then admitted he had spoken to him only for Neil to shout, "I know you did, it was me you were speaking to."

Neil did a number of voices on his phone calls. He got John Harrison once. John was going out to play for Australian side Gympie. Neil pretended to be an Australian coach saying John would be made welcome; he would be given a new car and a good contract. He enquired whether John could recommend a centre, perhaps one of his mates he played alongside because the team really needed a centre. He went on to say, "What about Loughlin, would he come?" He said that it would be company for John out there. John was made up and said that wouldn't be a problem. Neil was really spinning it now because he told John that we would both get jobs over there. He went on for ages ending with "Alright John, it's Neil here".

He would spend ages in the press box ringing random numbers. His favourite was to pretend to be a little old lady and that she had got the person's number out of the *St Helens Star* and was ringing about the sheepdog that was available because hers had just died. He'd start crying saying that the dog had been with 'her' for 15 years. The poor person on the other end would try and explain that she had got the wrong number; one bloke said he hadn't advertised a sheepdog but could get her one if she wanted.

Neil has always been one of my best mates; I was godfather to one of his lads. I even went to his house for Christmas dinner once. He still rings me up with different voices and I have no idea who it is. I have had to save his name and number to my house phone so I know it's him. It was worse when I was still at my mum's, she would tell me an Australian man or someone from Yorkshire Television had been on for me and I would have to tell her it was probably just Neil.

The league title came down to the last game of the 1992–93 season, we did our part by beating Widnes 29-18 at Knowsley Road, but Wigan also won, beating Warrington comfortably, and then beat Castleford at Central Park four days later, thereby taking the league ahead of us on points difference.

As a curtain raiser to the 1992 Premiership Final, the Second Division final was between Oldham and Sheffield Eagles. Tommy Martyn was playing for Oldham that day and had a cracking game. One of the Saints players said, "He'd be alright at our club, he'd fit in well with the team". I don't think Jonathan Griffiths was that pleased mind you. When Tommy signed for Saints in August 1993, it did take him a while to get going, but he turned into one of the best stand-offs the club has had. As a centre I loved having him playing inside me.

Tommy Martyn

"When I joined Saints from Oldham, a Second Division club, Lockers was an established international. I couldn't get over how friendly he was towards me. He welcomed me into the fold and he was one of the main jokers in the pack. As soon as he walked into the dressing room, everyone would be laughing. It's a friendship we've carried on well past our rugby playing days. He's always someone for whom I have a lot of time.

He's very laid back, once he's around friends he relaxes. When you speak to him, you wouldn't think he's a seasoned international who had played numerous tests for Great Britain. He's one of those people who wouldn't tell anyone what he had done to people who didn't know. He's a champion fellow.

He was great to play alongside, you only have to stand next to him to realise how big he is and how dominating he could be. If he wanted the ball, you just gave it to him. He would run straight and would make the players alongside him look absolutely brilliant. He was telling us where he wanted the ball and how he wanted it.

We went to play for the Great Britain Legends team in Hull once. There was me, Neil Holding and Lockers on a minibus coming back. Although he denies it, Lockers has a lisp. Now all three of us were going to do a little bit of after dinner speaking for Paul's football club. We were due to do around 10 minutes each. Paul was telling us how nervous he was and how he had been practising his speech to his dog when he was out walking it. He had been laughing to himself about his funny stories. Neil turned round to him and said, 'What sort of dog have you got Lockers?' Paul replied, 'You bastards, you know what sort of dog I've got, it's a th-pringer th-paniel'."

Possibly the favourite game of my career was the Premiership Final at Old Trafford at the end of the 1992–93 season when we beat Wigan 10–4. Before the game, Mike McClennan repeated what he had done at the same venue against the same opposition the previous year. He handed us an envelope with our opposite number's name on it and asked us to outperform him. The Premiership Final was a very tight game. My match-clinching try was a simple one, the ball came along the line and I had a stroll in from about five yards. Our defence was magnificent all game. Mike Riley was man-of-the-match for me although Chris Joynt was awarded the Harry Sunderland Trophy. It was probably one of my best defensive performances too. Everybody chipped in. The crowd were so loud towards the end. We only had a six-point cushion, we were just holding on and holding on. When the hooter went, all the Saints fans were jumping up and down. We had finally beaten Wigan in a final. It might have only been the Premiership, but it was still a big final.

It was a great team performance and a big feeling of relief. I had been struggling for form because of injuries and my testimonial was just starting. It was great to beat Wigan at Old Trafford and for me to get the winning try, good timing all round.

The 1993 Premiership Final

Kicking at goal at Old Trafford (Bernard Platt)

Celebrating a great victory against Wigan
(Courtesy *St Helens Reporter*)

Apparently, as we did our lap of honour, Shaun Edwards gestured to the Saints fans with four fingers signifying they had still won four trophies that year. That's just a Saints and Wigan thing. If I had won four trophies I'd have done the same. It was funny because the talk after the game wasn't about the win, but about a streaker who had invaded the pitch. He was blessed like a 1970s porn star. He was running at me, but fortunately George Mann got in his way. Two old ladies were sitting in the stand and one said: "He should be ashamed of himself" to hear the reply: "He's got nothing to be ashamed of." All the players' wives never mentioned the match, just the streaker and asked whether he part of the squad.

After collecting the trophy, we did a lap of honour and then formed two rows for the waiting press photographers. Kevin Ward came out on crutches to join the team shot. For reasons best known to himself, Bernard mimed giving Wardy a 'blow job' and was embarrassed to later find out that that moment had been caught on television.

He and Wardy had their own thing being in the forwards together, their own jokes and so on. Wardy was a legend. We made a video of the final for the team and all it showed was us lifting the trophy and Bernard's moment with Wardy.

Ricky Cowan was signed for the club in 1993 from New Zealand. He had originally come over with the 1985 New Zealand touring team. He had been a good prop back then. Mike McClennan signed him, he must have seen something in him, but he didn't break any pots for us. I had played against him in New Zealand on the 1988 tour; he was playing for Auckland at the time. Cowan was injured, I think he had four operations while he was over here. He got a car from the club as well. Blokes who had been at Saints for 10 years got precious little, he came over and was given a car and a nice house. He joined in the lap of honour with us when we won the Premiership in 1993.

Mark Bourneville was another Kiwi who came over; they used to call him 'Horse'. He was one of the strongest blokes I've ever seen, massive chest and hard as nails.

After that 1993 Premiership Final win, we had a good drink after the game, we left one of the forwards dressed as a policeman directing traffic in the middle of a road. My good mate Deano had been out with us. Deano used to come and watch Saints and knows a lot of the players who played under Mike McClennan. In fact, we ended up getting Deano a game. It was David Hulme's testimonial and he held a 'World Sevens' at Widnes. I wasn't meant to be playing because I was due to be having a hernia operation. Saints were one short, even with Deano, so I said I would play. The Saints team was Shane Cooper, Gary Connolly, Paul Forber, Alan Hunte, Phil Veivers, Brimah Kebbie, Deano and me. Shane got fined for playing me and I got fined for playing. It didn't help my cause that I broke my foot at the event. Deano had a great time and even managed to score a try.

Anyway, the night of our Premiership Final triumph, he had forgotten that he had promised to run his wife to Wigan the next morning. He had only been in bed about two hours when she started waking him up. He told her she would have to get the bus; she told him there was no chance because it was lashing it down with rain. He staggered out of bed, putting a pair of his wife's old jogging bottoms on. He coupled this with some old trainers with no laces and an old t-shirt. He had an old Capri and dropped her off at Wigan. On his way back, he felt his car shudder a bit and then noticed one of his front wheels bouncing down the road in front of him. It ended up through a field and down a ditch followed by the rest of Deano's car. He got out and looked around to make sure there was no-one about. He stank of ale, he had old tracksuit bottoms on covered in paint and trainers with no laces and the rain had made his t-shirt skintight. He started running down the road as if he was a jogger because his dad lived a mile down the road. The tracksuit bottoms started to sag and swing and felt about five stones in weight due to the rain. Lots of motorists on their way to work were beeping and waving to him. He banged on his dad's door. His dad didn't know whether to phone an ambulance or phone the AA for a new wheel. Deano ended up in bed for a week with flu. It was like that after some games, we would just carry on drinking.

It's a shame that Premiership Final was the last game of the season - we wanted to carry on playing! We thought of all the poor games we'd had; then had started to play well and wanted to keep going in the same vein. I felt that team could have been built on, but we slumped the year after and only finished 8th in the league. Losing Kevin Ward was a huge blow and Shane Cooper was approaching the veteran stage. If we could have added a bit more youth to the side, you never know. Having said that, two years later, in Super League, Saints ruled the roost anyway.

As with the 'Coors' game, we knew when we played at our best we could beat anybody. We proved it against Wigan, Widnes, Leeds and

56

Warrington. It was just the belief and the self-confidence as a team that was needed to make sure we could go out and do it. Wigan had that self-belief because of their lengthy run of success. They went onto the pitch never expecting to lose. Chris Joynt instilled a lot of belief into the side when he came to the club. After I left, he was clearly a leader. He shared a lot of Shane Cooper's characteristics, he led by example. The difference was Chris had better players around him.

I remember John Harrison and me watching the 'A' team on a Friday night at Saints. We had a 16-year-old at hooker who was outstanding. John said, "He's going to be a good 'un". It was a certain Keiron Cunningham. You can tell who the stars are going to be.

At the end of the season with Saints, we usually went to Tenerife or Magaluf. One year, nobody was interested so Les Quirk and I went to Ibiza. The first two days, we were sat with no top on in the sun supping pints. Les can sit out in the sun forever, I sadly cannot. I ended up in bed for the next four days with sunstroke. The last I saw of Les he was joining an '18–30' conga. One day he put some of his fishing bait under my pillow and I woke up with maggots round my head. I thought they were coming out of my body.

Another year, all the Saints lads went to Ireland, I had a broken arm then. Jonathan Griffiths was taking all the lads surfing, playing beach cricket and cliff diving, I just held all the coats and was the umpire for the cricket. I was all right at night when it came to the drinking though. We had gone in a car; there was Les, Mark Riley, Shane Cooper, Bernard and me. It turned out there was a wasp in the car with us. We pulled over to get it out of the car, but it stung Shane in the neck and to make matters worse, as we were moving the car, we ran over Shane's foot too. He was far from happy.

The 'Mad Mondays' got even madder when the game went full-time because nobody had to be up for work the next day. There were nights we would end up in the town centre with rags covering our bits. It was all lads together, good-natured fun.

St Helens RLFC 1994-95 – my last full season at the club.
(Courtesy Alex Service)

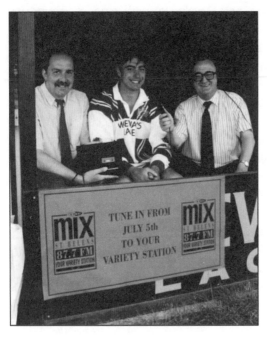

Facing the press – being
interviewed by Alex Service
and Denis Whittle in 1992
to publicise a local radio
project. (Courtesy Brian
Peers & *St Helens Star*)

5. Final days at Saints

The club parted ways with Mike McClennan in December 1993 after an incident with a supporter at Knowsley Road. Eric Hughes was the next head coach. He was a good coach but not, in my opinion, a manager. However, he was able to get us revved up. He would give you a rub before a game and be telling you to get stuck in. He used to end up hurting you half the time because he would take the skin off your legs. He was a fitness fanatic, but I thought wasn't good tactically. I didn't last long under him before being sold to Bradford. He had been hard as nails as a player, the 'Smiling Assassin' the lads used to call him. He struggled at Saints and I don't think the speccies took to him. He was a nice bloke though.

I had always got a good reception from the Saints supporters until I started getting niggling injuries – my confidence went a little bit and it seemed a section of the Popular Side were always on my back. If I missed a kick or whatever, they let me know about it, but I think every player goes through that. I ended up never being 100 per cent fit due to hernia injuries and a broken arm. Playing with injuries doesn't help, players shouldn't do it but they worry that while they are out, someone will take their spot. It wasn't nice to get stick. Players shouldn't read the papers anyway, but they sometimes published supporters' letters slating me. It's nice when you get good reports, but the other side of it can be difficult to take. It comes with the territory of being a professional sportsman though.

Paddy Loughlin
"I once said that the same supporters who call players rotten during the game are all over the same players in the bar afterwards."

Sometimes, it's down to the supporters a club attracts. When a club is successful they start to attract more supporters, some of whom don't really know much about the game. For example, in 2010 when Saints left Knowsley Road, they asked supporters to name the club's greatest ever 17 players. The bulk of players picked were from the modern era. Don't get me wrong, Saints have enjoyed a lot of success in recent years and had some great players, but a lot of the current supporters won't know about some of the legends from days gone by. Nobody from my era ever gets a look in. There have been some fantastic players in recent years. However, there is a feeling that with some people that rugby league started for them with the move to summer in 1996. Prior to that, the only players who really get remembered are in the 1960s and the van Vollenhoven era. My point is there were some genuine Saints legends in the 1970s and 1980s too.

It's hard listening to some of the comments from the crowd. It's more difficult and negative when it is your own fans doing it. I had my fair share of knockers, especially when I was playing with injuries. The worst thing players can do is start listening to the people slating them because it can affect their confidence and they can start to doubt themselves. Sometimes it did affect me. The fans have paid their money so are entitled to their opinion, but they're not in the team and have never pulled the famous shirt on. It's not as easy as it looks sometimes. I found it a bit depressing when I was injured and couldn't play to my full potential.

I remember one game where I had missed four kicks, I kicked the next one and some fans started shouting "Hallelujah", I couldn't win. My mates used to go the game and said there was one bloke who stood near them who was very anti-Loughlin. I could have beaten every opposition player on the pitch and scored by the side of the posts and he still would have shouted "You should have gone under the sticks Dobbin". You can't win with people like that though. Most of the Saints fans have always been good.

Later, the Bradford fans were brilliant with me during my two years there – same with Swinton and Huddersfield. The problem at Huddersfield was that the players couldn't really hear the support because there weren't that many there.

The Saints fans seemed to worship Roy Haggerty, Kevin Ward and Buffer. Maybe if I'd smacked a few players they would have liked me more. I've always found Saints fans brilliant on the whole though. It is great when people recognise me and say hello. I think St Helens people are just nice anyway. I might be biased, but that's how I feel.

Some away fans could be a bit much at times, I remember taking a kick for goal out wide at The Boulevard next to Hull's infamous Threepenny Stand. They were throwing toffees at me so I picked one up and started eating it. That just seemed to get them going again. Of course, straight from the kick-off, we scored in that corner again. I was expecting more than toffees heading my way the second time.

We played Leeds in the Challenge Cup semi-final in 1994 at Central Park. Leeds had a very good side at this time, including Ellery Hanley. Saints and Leeds were evenly matched in the semi-final, but two late Hanley tries won the match for them. We had played really well and would probably have beaten anyone else. They ended up getting hammered at Wembley so maybe it was a good thing. Wigan won the World Club Championship in Brisbane at the end of that season, and were virtually unstoppable at this point.

In 1993-94 I had a testimonial season. John Harrison gave me a lot of support. I always used to room with him when we were away with Saints because he was one of my best mates. He lived near me and we travelled together. I was his best man, the wedding was on a Friday and we played Workington on the Sunday. We both managed to have decent games somehow.

John is six feet nine inches tall, yet bought himself a Ford Fiesta. I would be sitting in it with him at six feet three inches. It was like Hightower from *Police Academy*. We would sometimes give Paul Doherty a lift, although with our bags there wasn't really much room. Often we would travel with Paul Doherty in the car boot.

John and I roomed together at Wembley one year. It was the night before the game and I could see the curtains moving. I thought the room was haunted. I walked over to close the windows, but they were already closed. I turned round and realised it was caused by big John snoring.

He came to most of my testimonial events with me. We had a race night at the Horseshoe pub in Parr. It was a Thursday night and we had a match on the Friday so most of the team couldn't come. John had a knock so he wasn't playing and agreed to support my race night. There was only John and me there with Dave Lane who did the race night. I thought I would have a laugh at John's expense. You had to pick a horse, and name both it and the owner. There were about 16 handy looking lads in the bar and I'm not sure how much interest they had in the race night. I decided to put down the name of one horse as 'All Parrers are soft bastards' owned by 'Mr John Harrison in the corner of the room'. Dave Lane was going through the horse names, saw this and started laughing. He announced it, on the microphone, to the entire pub. All eyes were on John, he just kept his head down. He saw the funny side though after he got out alive.

A testimonial season can be quite hard work. A lot of it was done by Katherine, Lenny Lowe who was the committee chairman, my dad, Dave Lane of Lane's Trophies, Denis Whittle, Alex Service, Jimmy Sullivan and George. They did all the organising and I just had to turn up to the events. Doing events twice a week then training and so on, did affect me. It was a long 12 months and with three months of my testimonial year left; I just couldn't handle it any more. My form dipped. It was lovely to get the money at the end of the day, but sometimes I did feel like I was begging.

People must have thought we were on fantastic money playing rugby and why did we want any extra? I ended up getting £35,000 which was a club record at the time and for which I will always be grateful. Bernard had his testimonial the year after and he broke the record. The thing was though, because we had a team of local lads who had stayed with the club, there was a testimonial every year and it was hard for supporters to keep putting their hands in their pockets.

It was around this time that Saints appointed a female physio, Jeanette Smith. There was a match at York where they only had one toilet in the dressing room; it was bizarrely situated right in the middle of the room. I am pretty sure this was one of Jeanette's first games as physio at the club. Before her we had Tim and Sammy Leyland as physios. Now it was a female physio, something only Widnes had tried before. The lads felt a bit strange about it at first – getting stripped off in front of her with most of them holding towels up. This day at York meant that all concerned got over it very quickly because everybody had to go in this little toilet and do their business while she strapped players up for the game ahead. You can imagine the smell; she must have wondered what she had joined.

In the end, we all got used to it. Jeanette was a brilliant physio; I saw more of her than anybody in the end because of my injury problems. I think most of the lads got a groin injury when she started. That phase soon passed.

While Eric Hughes was coach, we did a pre-season bike ride. The first year we just went to Southport. The players and our bikes were collected by Jeanette Smith in her horse box and that's how we travelled back. You couldn't make it up. The next year, Eric entered us into the Manchester to Blackpool charity bike ride. We all did it as part of pre-season training. Now 60 miles is a long way so we thought we would take some money with us in our bum bags and stop along the way for a drink or two. It was a red hot day. I recall me, Mike Riley, Les Quirk, Shane Cooper, Bernard Dwyer, Adam Fogerty and Ducky O'Donnell riding together. Shane's idea was for us to order blackcurrant and cider so that if Eric rode past he would think he were drinking blackcurrant. We stopped at about five pubs and ended up getting giddier and giddier. Two miles from Blackpool, we had had about nine pints each. Either Shane or Bernard had the idea that we should all strip off, put our t-shirts and shorts in our bum bag and cover our privates with our race number.

We all agreed this was a good idea, nipped into a shop for some sellotape and started the ride into Blackpool with just a race number protecting our modesty. It was funny at first but we then realised we had to cycle through Blackpool town centre to get to the finishing line at Stanley Park. It was a lovely day so there were families strolling through Blackpool only to see 10 rugby lads with their balls swinging off their bike seats. We weren't so bad from the front but from the back lifting off the seat it can't have been a pretty sight. I recognised one family I knew from Ashton and just tried to keep my head down.

We got to the park and, lo and behold, they had put up a stand with about 1,000 people watching complete with police and stewards. As we finished, the stewards waved us to one side and give us a good telling off. We then got another one from Eric. The one good thing was we were never asked to do it again.

Bobbie Goulding, Scott Gibbs and Apollo Perelini were big signings for Saints prior to the 1994–95 season. Eric told me he had spoken to Bobbie and he was happy for me to carry on with the goalkicking. I was having injury problems though, had been kicking for nearly 11 years and so handed over the kicking duties to Bobbie. He was a great kicker and probably more reliable at that point

When Bobbie is with rugby people, he is with his own and is a good laugh. A lot of things get blown out of proportion with Bobbie. He is famous in the sport and when you're recognised you can become a target for abuse from people on a night out. Bobbie is the type of bloke who can react to it. It's a shame what happened to him at Saints because he could have possibly gone on to attain Alex Murphy-status at the club. He took Saints back to the glory days again; and pretty much won the 1996 Cup Final on his own with his kicking.

I can't comment on what happened before he left the club because I wasn't there, but if he had a falling out with somebody, perhaps he could have kept it to himself and stayed at the club. He could have had more success at Saints. Having said that, he left and that opened the door for Sean Long and he didn't do too badly at Saints. He was another character; there must be something about scrum-halves.

Bobbie went to Huddersfield and it wasn't the same for him. Alex Murphy once said, "Once you leave Saints, you're on your way down." He was right in one way, although I did win the league with Bradford Bulls after leaving Knowsley Road.

I remember Apollo Perelini coming to the club for the first time in 1994; he looked like an American wrestler. It took him a little while to find his form because he had come from rugby union. With a name like Apollo and the nickname of 'The Terminator' he had to have something about him. He was a solid bloke, very quiet off the pitch and didn't drink. He was big mates with Vila Matautia.

We had been training one morning at Cowley Girls School. The afternoon was just a weights session, but there was a gap of an hour between sessions for dinner. Scott Gibbs was picking up a new Audi. I told him, "Yeah, great I will just put my sponsored Saints bicycle away." We went to the garage with him, all in our training kit and he offered to take us for a ride. There was me, Phil Veivers and Jonathan Griffiths in the car with him. "Let's go Blackpool," came the cry and off we went, all the while assuring Gibbs that Blackpool wasn't far and we'd be back in plenty of time for training. We had pictures of ourselves in full training kit riding 'The Big One' roller coaster in Blackpool while everyone at the club wondered where we were. We didn't do the weights anyway.

Apart from the new signings, we had other quality players in our ranks. Anthony Sullivan was one of the fastest wingers I ever played with. He came to the club from Hull KR in 1991 and was a flying machine. If he had a bit of space there was no catching him.

Alan Hunte was also a good player; I think he was more of a full-back than a winger. He was a player who could score from anywhere. It was strange though because he smoked like a chimney. He was built like a bodybuilder and thought he was the best dresser and dancer.

The first league game with the three new signings in the 1994-95 season was at home to newly promoted Doncaster. The supporters' expectations were sky high. In almost typical Saints fashion, we lost. It was a nightmare game. Rocky Turner, Jamie Bloem and Vila Matautia ripped us apart. I played full-back that day and I think overconfidence was our problem. The Doncaster side was all psyched up and caught us out. We got better as the season went on, but it was a bad start especially because it was followed by a heavy 31–10 midweek defeat at Warrington. That sticks in my mind because they kept kicking the ball past me and Sully for Richard Henare to score. He got four tries. I got one of ours.

The game started changing forever in 1995. It was decided to change from winter to summer rugby, starting in 1996. The 'Super League war' between television companies raged over in Australia and ultimately the English game signed with the Super League camp with more coverage on Sky Television. The money that flooded into the game was incredible; some young players made a lot and got loyalty bonuses. Most players were getting money for not doing anything at all really. It did seem to be a select few that were getting the money though. I thought it was certainly that way at Saints. The club must have had a say in who they wanted to keep and where these loyalty bonuses would go. A lot of players didn't get one including me and Bernard. It went crazy and some players were signing contracts, reneging on their word and keeping the money.

I liked the change to a summer season though because it was more enjoyable for players and supporters alike playing when it was a bit warmer. There used to be nothing worse than travelling to Yorkshire or Cumbria when it was freezing cold. I think it was the best thing that could ever have happened to the sport. Just look at how the skills of players have developed in the dry conditions.

Sky has been a fantastic broadcaster too; it has opened up the game to new audiences, particularly in London and France. It's gone from a flat-cap, Northern pastime to an entertaining family show.

There was a shortened Centenary season from August 1995 to January 1996 as clubs geared up for the start of the new era. During that season, Saints introduced a furry dog mascot called St Bernard, initially played by David Howes's son James. I thought it was good for the fans. They also had Neil Holding doing a 'catch the bomb' competition with supporters at half-time.

We played at Hull in the Regal Trophy in the Centenary season and I never knew that the game would be my last game for Saints. However, there were a lot of rumours that Saints were after Paul Newlove. My move away came out of the blue and it would have been nice to have played one more game for Saints and said my goodbyes.

65

My mate Deano.

Time off – with friends in York.

6. Great Britain

I remember my first training session with Great Britain and it was a big step up from club rugby. It was at Fartown; Mal Reilly was head coach at the time with Phil Larder supervising the backs during training. I remember how fast everybody seemed. I had Martin Offiah outside me. I thought that I was going to struggle to keep up with everybody. The pace of the international game is lightning fast and the more players are exposed to it, the better they become.

When I went to France with the under-21s in March 1987 I was playing alongside Gary Sanderson and Paul Bishop. Malcolm Reilly was coach at the time and we sat down in the hotel one night to tuck into big, thick steaks. They were delicious. We finished them and Malcolm said, "Now lads, that'll get you right for tomorrow, bit of horse in you". We'd all eaten horse.

A couple of weeks later I played for the Great Britain under-21s in the return match against France at Knowsley Road. I broke the points scoring record in that game with two tries and seven goals. Fellow Saint Kevin McCormack was my wing partner that day and he scored a try. I could have had a hat-trick, but put Kevin in for his try instead. He was built like a body builder and was quick and strong. He later had problems with his hamstrings. However, he was the best dancer I have ever seen in my life, he looked like he was floating. I only missed one goal that game and it was great to do it in front of my home crowd. I broke a few records in the early part of my career. Broadcaster Stuart Pyke always used to ask me questions about records coming along for me to break and I would always give the same answer about it being a team game and so on. He could have just used a tape of me saying that every week. Stuart used to do the Saints newsline service in those days; he does darts commentary now as well as rugby league.

When I went back to France with the senior Great Britain side, my dad took a group from his pub. Some of the under-21 players who had gone over went on a bit of a rampage. The police started grabbing everyone who had rugby shirts on, including supporters, and locked them up. Some of my dad's group missed the train, it cost him a fortune to get them all back home. The RFL wouldn't help and I believe my dad fell out with them over the incident.

Great Britain under-21 squad 1987.

Playing for Great Britain in France one year, their winger hit me like an Exocet missile and I suffered a dead leg. It was so painful I thought I had broken it. It took me some time to start feeling right again. There was scar tissue and it felt like I had a pulled muscle all the time. I was in the treatment room at Saints and Bernard asked, "Is it sore that?" as he slammed his hand down on it hard. It took four men to peel me down from the ceiling.

Playing against France wasn't too bad. It was a step up facing New Zealand and then a huge step up against the Australians. The best way to explain it is that sometimes I could afford to switch off in club rugby, but not against the Australians. Everything happened at breakneck speed all the time.

In my time there were no cliques in the international setup, everybody just got on with each other. I mingled with everybody. We used to socialise together. A tour was a good 13 weeks learning curve. We bump into each other at various dinners and are still friends. We still have a laugh.

It was sometimes a little difficult gelling with your winger at international level defensively. It was easier in attack because everything came from the half-backs such as Shaun Edwards, Andy Gregory, Garry Schofield or Ellery Hanley. I would time my runs based on what the halves were doing and making sure my winger wasn't going to overrun me. I partnered some great wingers at international level, including Martin Offiah, Henderson Gill, Dessie Drummond and Gerald Cordle. Offiah made his debut with me in January 1988 against France.

I was glad to play with Dessie Drummond at international level as it was a whole lot more fun than playing against him. Off the field, he was a lovely bloke talking in his Bolton accent. I played in a legends match against Australia with him a few years ago and he hadn't changed.

He used to target my ribs when he tackled me, especially at Wilderspool with its narrow pitch. I would get the ball, the centre Paul Cullen or Ronnie Duane would let me get around the outside then Dessie would hit me. I used to dread playing against him; I cringe about it even now.

I had been picked for Great Britain to play against France and there were rumours that I was in line for selection for the 1988 tour. Due to injuries, I knew there was a full-back spot open for the tour party, and I had been playing there for Saints.

Paddy Loughlin

"I told Paul he would go on the Great Britain tour and he didn't believe me. This was because Murphy had given him a rocket up and down the place one game after he had played full-back and had knocked on under the posts. Of course, Paul did go on the 1988 tour and the story went from there."

When I got the call to be told I was selected for the tour, I couldn't believe it. It was the best 13 weeks of my life. I learnt a lot about the other players. For example, Karl Fairbank, a farmer, was sharing with another farmer Paul Dixon, and I walked in their room during the tour. I went in to get something from their room to hear Karl on the phone to back home. "Is Daisy all right?" he was asking. "Give her a kiss and tell her I'll be back soon." I apologised to him for walking in on this tender conversation between him and his daughter. He said, "Na, it was one of the calves." I don't think he had been far from saying, "Put her on the phone to me."

The rugby was brilliant, I had a really good tour and I was voted man-of-the-tour. I had some great games and played some good rugby. There was the other side to the tour as well, including going to the Great Barrier Reef. We had a good day there having a few drinks.

Once I'd had enough of the sun, I headed down into a café that had a huge glass wall looking underneath the ocean. There were two elderly, well-to-do English ladies there. They asked me if I was with the rugby team and I told them that I was. They told me they couldn't believe how well behaved we all were and that they had been surprised because they had expected us to be very rowdy. They told me we all had impeccable manners. They didn't know there were two players standing behind them waving to me with their trunks in their hands and their tackle wafting about. I made my excuses and left.

There was racism in the crowd back in the 1980s towards the black players. I was never racist; I used to share a room with Phil Ford. He was one of the liveliest blokes you could meet. We were paired up and roomed together on tour as the organisers wanted to mix us all up. Fordy would go out on the ale and would tell me in his lilting Welsh accent, "I've left you a little cigarette at the side of your bed." I would go out and have a puff on the balcony. There was never any racism among the players. The shouts from the crowd were probably because they were good players and were doing damage.

We had been leading the first test in 1988 6–0 and ended up losing 18–6. They had a quality side including Wally Lewis, Paul Vautin and so on. However, Ellery Hanley was one of the best players to play the game in my eyes. I'll never forget that first test against Australia. His performance that day was quite simply the best I've ever seen anybody play. He was up against Wally Lewis, but took everybody on. His tackling was great, he was strong and he was fast. He may not have been the most skilful ball-handler, but everything else he did was brilliant. He is the best player I have ever seen, played with and against. I've seen how hard he trains first-hand. He is a nice bloke too. I found that he was a quiet man who kept himself to himself.

One story that happened with Roy Haggerty was on the 1988 tour to Australia. We got off the plane and were interviewed by the Australian press. They gave Roy a big build up by saying he was the Great Britain danger man, the hard man of rugby league and that he was going to talk to the press. The first question they asked him was where did he come from and he replied, "Top of Elephant Lane," as if the Australians were going to say, "Oh yeah, what number?" They asked him where that was and he told them it was, "A suburb of Thatto Heath."

Playing for Great Britain against New Zealand, 1988 World Cup match.

Being presented with the man-of-the-match award after playing for Great Britain against France (Varley Picture Agency).

Going to Australia and seeing how they invest in sport really opened my eyes. When we went on tour, we used to stay in Manly. There was a local rugby union club there and the facilities they had would put Saints to shame. This was just a small, amateur rugby union club. When Australia does a sport, they do it properly. They make sure people enjoy their sport although I accept that the weather helps them. They don't take any shortcuts. If they identify sporting talent at a young age, they put them into academies – that's why they have so many good players. They make sure everything is right for the players to develop.

One great memory from that tour was the best try I made at international level. It was the famous try scored by Henderson Gill in the third test, which we won. It was our first victory against the Australians since 1978, and we had a depleted team because of injuries. I had been doing big kicks during the test series because I found I could kick the Australian balls for miles. During the game, I got the ball and was about to kick. I saw their prop, Sam Backo, racing towards me and didn't fancy being hit by him so I dummied, went round him, then handed players off as I switched the ball from hand-to-hand. I thought to myself "I'm never going to reach the line" and spotted Henderson Gill outside me. Gary Jack was ahead of us and I thought Hendy had a better chance than me so gave him the ball. Off he went to score in the corner topped off by his famous boogie dance. Most of the players went over to Hendy, but the two Hulme brothers came and patted me on the back which was nice.

It was a cracking try accompanied in the same game by a Mike Gregory try of some quality. Then there was the Phil Ford's 'He's a stepper, Ford' try. Great memories of a wonderful win. All the tries we scored in that test win were outstanding; the combination of the two Gregory's for Mike's try and of course Phil Ford's weaving effort. That was a brilliant touring side. There are not many players who can claim they have beaten the Australians in their own backyard. It would have been ever better if it had been a series win.

Mal Reilly had told us before Papua New Guinea and the other warm-up games in 1988 to get the ball and turn the full-back round with a long kick. Australia were so dangerous in our half so he wanted us to keep them penned in their own half.

I used to knock about with the Hulme brothers on tour, they were good lads. Well, until you played against them. If I cracked one, I knew it was only a matter of time before the other brother got me. They used to give me a crack in the tackle. If I did it back to them in a tackle, they would come over all hurt and offended, saying, "What's wrong with you? I thought we were friends."

David was actually a quiet lad on tour, he would take the mickey all the time, mind you. He was very competitive. I wish I had had a brother in the same team when I was playing.

Paddy Loughlin

"Paul made some great friends. One thing I was made up with was when he was on tour he got on really well with the Widnes lads. Before he went on the tour, I had told him, 'Enjoy yourself by all means, but remember what you are out there to do'. He knocked about with the two Hulme brothers and Paul became known as the 'Widnes clone'. I was made up when he got 'player's player-of-the-tour', you know when you get a player's award you have done something to deserve it. We had all top quality backs at that time but could never really match the Australians in the pack. It's no coincidence to me that New Zealand have started to have some success now as they have some big, handy lads in the pack. The stand out memory from that 1988 tour is of course Paul breaking through from his own 25 and giving it to Henderson Gill. The rest, as they say, is history. It's still a try that gets shown to this day. To have the respect of your fellow internationals is a big thing. They're always glad to see him at the reunion dinners they have."

Wally Lewis was one of the all-time greats playing in that test series for Australia and it was gratifying to see him name me in his all-time best Great Britain team in his book.

Some of the local games on that tour were top quality too: the Northern District, in particular as it was their test match. They were all very hard games. All the Australians wanted a crack at the Poms and all the touring players were fighting for test jerseys. Lots of players picked up injuries including Lee Crooks, Andy Platt and Les Holliday. There was such competition for places and it made the players raise their game.

On the Wednesday before the first test match we played Manly and got beaten 30–0. Roy Haggerty was sin binned in that game. Later, we played a Presidents' XIII at Canberra and faced what was practically a test side. That was also the game where a dog ran on the pitch. I scored a try in the corner, put the ball down to take the conversion and a dog ran on. Every time I went to take the conversion, the dog ran towards the ball and the crowd went mad cheering. There were about 20,000 there and they had a good laugh. I picked up a ball and booted it out of the ground. The dog hared after it, jumped over a wall and left the ground. I quickly got another ball from the ball boy and took the kick. It sailed between the sticks.

New Zealand beat us 12−10 in a World Cup game towards the end of the tour. I scored a try, but missed two kicks in a gale force wind. The final game was against Auckland and I had the worst haircut of my life. I went for a flaptop like Vanilla Ice later did. The barber asked me if I wanted it a bit shorter so I said 'Yes'. He gave me a proper bald patch on top with hair sticking up at the front with a little bit at the side. I asked Mal Reilly if I could play in a scrum cap, but he said no. I ended up putting boot polish on my head to cover the bald patch, but during the game it got rubbed off. The next day in the paper, there was one picture of me with the caption 'The badger'. Andy Gregory still talks about that haircut to this day.

Andy Gregory

"Paul's haircut in New Zealand on the 1988 tour was horrendous. To be honest, it's the worst haircut I have ever seen in my life. I said to him, "Lockers, you're representing your country at the weekend, you're going to have to do something about it." He asked whether he could wear a cap. I thought he meant a skull cap and said that he never usually wore one. He meant a bob cap that he would tape to his head. We managed to get through it.

In my eyes, he typifies what sport is all about. He always had a smile on his face, he's a loveable lad who hasn't got a bad word about anybody. He just gets on with it.

He was such a naturally talented player. In our team talks at Wigan, Lockers would always be upmost in our thoughts. We would say that Saints had strength in depth but you had to watch out for Paul Loughlin and that's what we did. They had other good players in key positions, but Lockers was always a player who everybody admired and had respect for.

He's never changed, he's just a lad who gives 100 per cent for his club. He is Saints through and through, he was always a Saints man. I know how proud I was to play for my country and I know how proud Paul was to play for his country."

I think they should try and bring those tours back, that time away together, that's how you win test matches. You need time to get used to your international team-mates and to get to know them properly. The shortened tours in recent years haven't worked, witness the Leeds-Saints cliques in 2008 in Australia. We had no cliques on the 1988 and 1992 tours. Yes, there was competition and fighting for places, but we all pulled together. That showed in the results. I've never experienced anything like it before and just wanted to do it again. I did in 1992, but came back with a broken arm. Being man-of-the-series on that 1988 tour is something I will never forget.

Maurice Lindsay was the tour manager for those tours and he was a nice bloke. He organised everything well for the players. He made Wigan what they are. If you ask most players what they think of Lindsay, they will tell you he is a good bloke. I see Andy Gregory sometimes and he always speaks well of Lindsay.

I began to establish myself as an international player in 1988. I lined up opposite Mal Meninga each time in the tests. The Australians have the huge advantage of using the intense three-match battleground of State of Origin as preparation for test rugby. We tried it over here with the Lancashire and Yorkshire Rodstock 'War of the Roses' matches. With the Lancashire team, some players pulled out before the games. I remember playing in Yorkshire and I was marking Garry Schofield who had moved to centre to allow Ellery Hanley the stand-off position. All the Yorkshire lads were well up for it, they had real pride in the jerseys. I thought I would fly into Schofield the first chance I got; he just sidestepped me and went the full length of the pitch to score. Doug Laughton was Lancashire coach at the time and was good with me. The matches themselves never really got caught on and the concept didn't work. There seems to be a different mindset in Australia compared with Super League clubs, I'm sure you'd see players pulling out left, right and centre if it was tried now. It shows how strong the game is over there that Adrian Morley went over, developed his game and is still a top forward in Super League to this day. That's why I'm glad Sam Burgess and Gareth Ellis have gone over. Playing at a better standard can only improve the England side in my opinion.

At international level now, I think we have the forwards to match anybody and some good backs. Unfortunately, I think the Australians could field about three top sides. We had our best chance against the Australians in 1990. We had some of the best British players ever, including Lydon, Edwards, Gregory, Schofield and Hanley.

In 1989 New Zealand came over for a three-match test series. Great Britain lost the first test at Old Trafford. I remember marking Dean Bell that day. The Kiwis had a good side. In the second test, Steve Hampson got sent off for butting and I got moved to full-back. Funnily enough, Steve played the following day for Wigan and got sent off again for butting. Andy Goodway moved out to centre and kept Kevin Iro quiet. He just smashed him all day; they were team mates at Wigan which may have added some spice. Andy was quick enough to play centre anyway. We won 26−6 despite being down to 12 men. The deciding test was played at Central Park and we won 10−6 on a sludgy, wet day. After the game, Steve Hampson, Andy Gregory and I went to a pub in Ashton to watch Deano's band play. We ended up with our Great Britain ties around our heads. Being involved in a Great Britain series win against a top side was fantastic. Our skipper was Mike Gregory and David Hulme had a brilliant series.

If it hadn't been for injuries, I would have gained more test caps. I was picked for the Wembley test in 1990 against Australia when we won. I went over on my foot, hurting my ankle while training at St Helens amateur club UGB and that put paid to my test spot. I came on as a substitute in the second test at Old Trafford and I scored an interception try.

I scored that try in the second test and Paul Eastwood offered me the ball to kick at goal. You can never turn the clock back but I wish I had accepted now instead of turning him down. To be fair, he had been kicking them from everywhere and I was coming back from my ankle injury, I had only played against Neil Holding's Rochdale. I think Mail Reilly blames me for the loss in his book. I might have missed the kick anyway, and then he really would have blamed me. After I scored at Old Trafford against Australia, their coach Bobby Fulton referred to me as a 'giraffe'. I think it was because of my long legs and arms and the way I reached out for the ball. When I scored the try, perhaps I should have gone closer to the posts. However, out of the corner of my eye I saw Laurie Daley coming across. I thought it was still close enough to the posts for Paul Eastwood to have kicked the goal. If he had, it would have been 12-10; as it was; after I scored it was 10-10.

If we had kept our line towards the end, we could have hung on to draw. Lee Jackson came out of the line, took the dummy off Ricky Stuart, suddenly the ball was in Meninga's hands and he was powering away. That's the closest we've come as a nation to a series win, because we could have won at Old Trafford and they beat us easily in the third test to clinch another series triumph.

Some players go through their whole career and are lucky enough never to suffer a major injury. The most serious ones I had were probably breaking my right arm twice. The first time, I had a steel plate put in it; I played a few games for Saints then went on the 1992 tour after also undergoing a double hernia operation which had caused me to miss the 1991 internationals.

I was picked for the first test against Papua New Guinea. Their players were only small, but had heads as hard as bowling balls. Andy Platt had warned me "whatever you do, no head high tackles against them, and you'll regret it." We then played a match before the first test against Australia. During the test, I felt a pain shoot up my body from my hernia. I had to go off and could hardly move for around half an hour. I found out when I came home that I had suffered another tear so had to have another operation.

After the first test we had a midweek game. Three of our forwards were having a competition during this game to see who could hit the hardest with their elbows. The Australians had brought this treatment on themselves because they had all been trying to take our heads off in the midweek matches. I came on as a substitute in the first half of this match, against the New South Wales Country team. I got the ball, saw a big forward running at me and thought I would smash him with my elbow. I sent him flying and threw the ball away. One of our forwards patted me on the back saying "Well done Lockers". I looked down at my arm and knew it had gone again. The plate had made my arm weaker, it was the end of my tour and I had to go home.

Paddy Loughlin

"I organised a tour with my pub at the time, The Rifle, to go and support Great Britain on the 1992 tour. The day we arrived though was the day Paul was going home injured. We arrived just after midnight and we were stopping in Cairns. The first person I met was

Dennis Hartley, former Castleford and Great Britain prop, who I knew from my playing career. He said, 'Bad news Paddy, your lad's going home'. I said, 'You're joking aren't you?' He told me that Paul had got hurt in a match and it was the end of his tour. I went to reception and asked them to put me through to the Queensland Rugby League. In turn, they put me through to Sydney and I managed to speak to Paul just before he was due to leave. It was a great disappointment. The injury occurred in a game where Paul played to help the team out. It even stopped Paul getting a job in the police force after that due to his medical record."

My arm was operated on with the plate removed and replaced by bone grafts off my hips which were grafted on. After that, it really knocked my confidence. It was always in the back of my mind that one more break and my career was probably over. It affected my tackling to be honest. I went through a period from 1990 to the time where I left Saints where I always seemed to have some sort of injury.

John Huxley
"I shall never forget Paul Loughlin's face the night after he broke his arm on the 1992 tour of Australia. My attempts at consolation late in the evening after a long stay at the bar were not particularly articulate. But anger never crossed Paul's expression once and the pain of the situation was mirrored in his eyes. Who said professionals just don't care? Nevertheless Paul had enough professionalism even at that dark moment not to be rude. His injury was a bitter blow not just to him, but the whole party."

Martin Offiah
"Paul Loughlin and I made our international debuts together back in 1988 and along with Darren Wright and Gene Miles must take the lion's share of credit for many of the things I have achieved in my career. Not only is Paul a genuine world-class centre, but he is also a good friend and a very funny guy, one of the true personalities in this great game."
(Interviews from The Paul Loughlin Souvenir Testimonial Brochure)

Papua New Guinea was an experience in itself. The first time I went, there were three other Saints players: Andy Platt, Paul Groves and Roy

78

Haggerty. Andy Gregory was on the tour and he had been before so knew what to expect. We couldn't go out of our hotel at night; there were problems with murders and rapes. While we were there, a bus had been stopped, the coach driver shot and some female passengers raped.

In the daytime, it was a little different. There was a sports shop we were safe to walk around in. Andy Gregory knew where there was a yachting club where the ex-pats used to go for a drink. We used to get taxis there and have a pint.

Training there was like being in a sauna, it was so humid. The pitches were rock hard. Their supporters would touch us and call us 'Lion' which was more than little strange. We played the test there in Port Moresby which was a little ground with a small stand. The supporters were in the trees watching. Luckily, I wasn't there for the 1990 tour when there had been a riot with CS gas sprayed.

We flew to a place called Lae where we played a Northern/Highland Zones side. There were two little planes to get us there; one for the kit and one for the players. I was wedged between the two pilots, petrified. Here we were flying through the clouds and between mountain tops; it was like something out of *Indiana Jones*. I wouldn't like to spend two weeks' holiday in Papua New Guinea, but what an experience it was. I wouldn't have been able to have done that if it wasn't for rugby. When I went back in 1992 I knew what to expect.

My mate Deano ended up getting up involved in my international career. He used to come everywhere with me, after I lost my driving licence and would take me places. He had a big Cadillac at the time which he used for weddings. Great Britain were training once at Castleford: Ellery Hanley turned up in a Black Audi, Martin Offiah pulled up in a black BMW. They were getting lots of attention from the press there. Deano pulls up in this big, white Cadillac with his driver's hat on like a chauffeur. I sat in the back, reading a newspaper. He pulled in, got out and opened the boot to get my bag out. By now, all the press had come over. He opened the door for me saying, "Here is your bag Mr Loughlin," and all the photographers were snapping away. People must have thought I'd done all right for myself and that Saints had started paying proper money.

After one test match against Australia that Deano took me to, there was a big dinner which Sky Sports were filming. Phil Larder and most of the players knew Deano because he was often around so he got invited to the dinner. Deano was also in a 1970s style rock band that Andy Gregory and other players had seen. His band performed at a number of players' testimonial events and recently appeared for the Steve Prescott Foundation's 'Band in the Park' event. When we later watched Sky's coverage of the dinner, it was all about Deano and how much food he could eat, I didn't even get a sniff. He later got a Harley Davidson for Andy Gregory; I think Andy needed a stepladder to get on it though. Deano got to know everybody; he was 'Mr Rugby League' for a spell.

Another time, Andy Platt had just passed his driving test so he, Kevin McCormack and I took my car because I had one, but didn't have a licence. We were due in Lilleshall for a 26-man Great Britain training day. It was an old Fiat Strada. We ended up getting lost and didn't think we could get there so Andy suggested we go Alton Towers instead. Andy asked how much money we had on us. I had four quid, typically for them both Andy and Kevin had no money at all. When we arrived, it was eight quid a person to get in. So it was no Lilleshall training and no rollercoasters at Alton Towers.

7. Off to Odsal

It was strange how the Bradford move came about. Saints had a midweek evening game at Odsal on 17 November. I remember warming up before the game alongside Bernard - it was freezing and I remarked: "I wouldn't want to play here every week." Bernard agreed with me, after all, Odsal had previously been a council rubbish tip. *The Hustle* by Van McCoy boomed incongruously across the tannoy over the cold, winter air. It couldn't have been less like a disco. There seemed to be no-one in the ground apart from the Saints fans who had made the trip. We had a couple of players sent off but still managed to win. Simon Knox cracked my rib during the game which is an injury that the physios can't really do much about. And yet two weeks later, I was there signing for the club after saying it had been too cold for me.

As an opposition player it was a horrible ground to go to, especially in winter. Half the time, the posts couldn't be seen because it was either foggy or driving rain. They also had the biggest forwards in the world over the years including players such as Kelvin Skerrett, Jeff Grayshon, Karl Fairbank, David Hobbs and Brendan Hill. It was a tough place to kick goals at as well. Wigan was another ground where goalkicking could be tricky because the posts seemed narrower the higher they went up.

I was gutted at leaving Saints and couldn't believe it was happening. I thought I was going to be at the club forever. I had just signed a new Super League contract for them. I had been offered £25,000 a season under the terms of the new deal. I had asked if I could have a car included. I received a phone call a week later asking me to come to the club. I assumed it was to do with my request for a car. I got to the club and saw that Sonny Nickle and Bernard Dwyer were there. I asked Bernard what was going on and he told me, "Paul Newlove's coming here; you, Sonny and I are going to Bradford." I thought he was joking, but he assured me he was serious. Bernard was delighted; Saints hadn't offered him a great deal despite him being arguably our most consistent player at the time. Bradford had put together a good deal for him and he was itching to take it. He urged me to accept the move, saying: "You have to sign otherwise I won't be able to go." I was standing there, devastated at the news and Bernard followed up with: "Come on, sign. We'll have a laugh."

Bernard Dwyer

"After spending so many years at Saints together, I remember on a Monday night being told to go down to the club. I thought I might be signing a new contract. When Paul and Sonny joined me, we learned we were all being sold to Bradford, we were all gutted really. We just made a decision to make the most of it. We were absolutely devastated, but when we got to Bradford and found out what it was all about, it was a really great time to be at the club."

I was told I was to leave by Eric Hughes the coach, Eric Ashton the chairman and David Howes, the chief executive. I knew Howes from his time as Great Britain team manager; he'd only been at Saints for two weeks when he sold me. When I went in to see Howes and Hughes, the way they were sitting there told me something was up. They told me Paul Newlove had signed so I said, "What if I stay?" They told me they would just play me in the 'A' team. They said they had Gibbs and Newlove and I would go in the 'A' team. They weren't going to pay Gibbs and Newlove the sort of money they were on for them to be sitting in the 'A' team. They could easily fob me off and stick me there though. I was devastated after all those years, especially having grown up as a supporter of the club.

It did turn into a good deal for everybody. I was bitter and twisted when I was playing, but as soon as I packed in, the bitterness was gone. I looked out for the results because some of my mates played for Saints. It hurt at the time though; it felt like losing your job. But I wasn't the first and I certainly won't be the last.

Neil Holding

"Paul leaving Saints to go to Bradford was a bitter pill for him to swallow. He turned up on my doorstep that night absolutely broken-hearted. I didn't know what was going on. He just said, 'They've sold me Neil'. It reduced the big fella to tears so I sat him down and told him: 'These things happen. Go and make a name somewhere else, it's no use dwelling on it.' He took it on board."

It was a good move for all parties in the end. Saints got a great player in Newlove, the three of us played at Wembley twice and won Super League. We also went to Australia on a fantastic three-week holiday also known as the World Club Challenge. It took me about a week to recover from that.

When I moved to Bradford, there were barely 3,000 fans watching them as Bradford Northern. Come the summer era with the advent of Bullmania and Odsal was packed. Bernard Dwyer and I transformed that club. That's what Bernard says anyway.

I took a two-year deal with the Bulls, Bernard signed for three years and Sonny for four. I was gutted while Bernard was banging on about the sponsored car Bradford were going to give him.

I disguised my voice and phoned Bernard up, pretending to be a sponsor at Bradford. I told him that there was a top-of-the- range Rover waiting for him with free petrol, tax and insurance... on the condition that it had Bernie the Bull painted on the side and a picture of a Bull. Bernard hates being called Bernie for a start. He went along with it though. I told him it was me and he put the phone down on me. He called me back 10 minutes later calling me a "fucking bastard".

After spending so long at Saints, my first day at Bradford was like the first day at school; it was weird. We had to do a press event when we got there. It wasn't as big as Saints did with Newlove arriving and coming out of the back of a security van. We just got out of the back of Bernard's Ford Focus. There was no crowd to welcome us. When we got into the club, they gave us some club jumpers to wear for the press photos. They were black jumpers with a picture of a bull on them. We had to put them on and then make bull horns over our heads with our fingers. I felt embarrassed. When it came time to sign our contracts, Chris Caisley and Peter Deakin were there from the club. We took it in turns to sign and as Bernard was signing his contract and answering questions from Caisley and Deakin, I strolled behind the officials and started pulling faces at Bernard. He burst into laughter to puzzled questions of "What's the matter Bernard? Do you find it funny that you're signing for a big club?" Bernard had to apologise. He tried to beat me up when we got outside.

The players made us very welcome. I knew some of them, including Brian McDermott, Jon Hamer, Robbie Paul and Simon Knox. Simon lived in Golborne so we ended up travelling to the club together with Matt Calland. I had been on tour with Karl Fairbank. Roger Simpson was also there, but didn't figure too much because he had a job on the ground staff and didn't want to commit to going full-time as a player. I had known Roger since very early in my career when we had played for the Great Britain Colts together.

I had first met Bernard at Saints when we were 16. Because he had a beard though, I thought he was about 30 years old. We really had a laugh when we went to Bradford with all the time spent travelling over together. We would pick Matt Calland up on the way and take the mickey out of him. One day we were coming back from Bradford, it was freezing; it must have been about minus 10. We were in a Rover with an electric sliding sunroof. Matt was sitting in the back and we dared him to stand up with his head out of the sunroof to see how long he could last. Bear in mind, we were doing around 70 miles an hour down the M62 at the time. Matt stood up with his head out of the sunroof and as I had expected, Bernard shut the sunroof on his head. We took him home like this all the way to Shaw. When he got out his face was blue, his hair was solid and he couldn't close his mouth.

Odsal was great in the summer. We finished third in 1996 and top in 1997. They had a different approach to the presentation of the game. As the 1996 season went on, music was played after we scored and there were dancers on the scoreboard. Bradford also had motorbikes and horses going round the old speedway track as part of the entertainment. The mascot Bullman used to come for a drink with the players after the game, out of his costume obviously. Bradford really took to the new summer era on and off the field with 'Bullmania'. I really enjoyed it; it was very different from how Odsal had been in winter. They made it a big family show. It showed in the attendances, Bradford gave free tickets to children which I think all clubs should do. I know it doesn't bring in any money, but the parents still have to buy a ticket to take them and this builds the crowds and builds a good atmosphere. We had some good groups on before matches too, T'Pau performed once while we were warming up. I used to like them when I had a 'tache.

It all worked though as the crowd got behind the team and the team played well. I have always said that a good, positive crowd behind the team lifts the players' moods, and when the mood is right it builds confidence and when the players' confidence is high they can do anything. It all comes together.

A lot of it was down to Peter Deakin and what he brought back from America when he and Brian Noble went over there to see how their sports operate. He made the entertainment side of the game what it is today. It also led to me making another foray into the recording studio as the players recorded and released *Running with the Bulls*. Two songs can't be bad considering I can't sing, I've got a lisp and have big teeth. My first 'single' had been for Saints at Wembley, and is covered in that chapter.

I even had to pose for a Bradford Bulls calendar that was sold at the club. A young girl who was working at the club at the time walked in as I was getting ready and saw me in the nude. I'm not sure who was more embarrassed! I joked to my team mates that my month should be titled 'butcher's dog' because I was all 'ribs and dick'.

Graham Bradley was a good player; he had come over from Australia a few seasons before to join Castleford. He had played in the Challenge Cup Final when they lost to Wigan. He was a bit like Shane Cooper because he was a leader. He could play stand-off, second-row or centre. I learnt new ideas from him even at that stage of my career because he could run brilliant lines. He just fitted in with the type of team that Bradford had.

My third game for the Bulls was in London against the Broncos. Bernard had missed a couple of games with an ankle injury. The game was played at Charlton FC's ground, The Valley. We stayed over and some of the lads went out into London. Bernard had decided to stay at the hotel because he wanted to ice his ankle. I volunteered to stay with him. We were the only two from the squad who didn't go out. We decided we would stay off the booze so Bernard could get his ankle sorted. Anyway, after a while, I told Bernard I fancied just one pint. He looked at it and said: "That looks nice". I told him because there was nobody else present he could have a couple. He agreed and that was it: the worst thing we ever did. We ended up having about 15 pints. As the night went on, dribs and drabs of other players arrived back at the hotel and would buy us another pint. On it went. We had spent the night arguing between the two of us who was hardest, who had been the best player, who was the best goalkicker, as the two of us did whenever we were together. We thought we had better get back to our room. We got in our room, no sooner had I looked round than Bernard was stark naked. All I could see was his big, hairy body. He said: "Loughlin, I've always wanted a do with you." I asked him if I had to strip off and he said I did. So, there we were, both naked, it was like a scene from *Women in Love* where Oliver Reed and Allan Bates have a naked fight in front of a log fire.

Bernard and I wrestled for what felt like two hours. We smashed both beds and pulled the curtains down. Bernard was really going for it, sat on my chest while he was punching me, with his balls dangerously near my face. I managed to swing my legs back and knock him off me. I told him, "That's it Bernard, we'll call it a draw". He agreed.

In the morning, we had a pool session in the hotel at 9am. At 9.10am, Bernard and I were still asleep. Our phone rang; it was the assistant coach, Matt Elliott. He told us we needed to get down because all the other lads were stretching in the pool. I told him we wouldn't be long. At 9.30am, we came down and I told Bernard there was no way I fancied doing any swimming. I felt terrible. Bernard pulled his shorts right up and stuck his belly out. We walked right past the squad unrecognised and headed for the sauna. My view was if we were going to get told off, we might as well sit in the sauna. Nobody said anything.

On the flight back from London, Bernard and I were pretty sheepish, trying to keep a low profile. All the other lads were laughing at us. Brian Smith asked if he could have a word with both of us. He told us we would both be put on the transfer list and be fined £500. Bernard was devastated, but managed to sweet talk him round. I think he was just trying to scare us. It was the last wrestling match we ever had. They tried to stop us rooming together, but they never did.

It was strange coming back to Knowsley Road with the Bulls. All the team stayed at Haydock apart from me as it made more sense for me to stay at home because I was still living in the town. I met up with the Bradford squad, trained with them then headed home. I made my own way to the ground, tried to get into the club car park and the steward told me I couldn't park there. I said that I was playing that day. He asked what my name was and I replied, "I've only been gone three months." Another steward came over, saw me and waved me in. The first one must have been new at the club. Bernard, Sonny and I all got a good reception from the Knowsley Road supporters.

I really enjoyed my time at Bradford; I was injury free and built up a great understanding with Robbie Paul. There was a little play we called 'stand up'. He would run across the pitch with the ball - he was that quick he would run around the stand-off – he would then straighten up and the centre would be in two minds whether to stay with me or go for Robbie. As soon as the centre moved, Robbie would give me the ball and I would either be through the gap or put my winger away, usually Jon Scales. Nobody would stop him when he was on the burst, all 17½ stone of him. His career had taken off at Bradford after joining from Leeds. A few players revived their careers at Bradford including James Lowes, Graham Bradley and Matt Calland.

There was also Robbie Paul breaking through. I remember playing against Robbie when I was at Saints and he had just started to get picked. He was playing centre against me, Anthony Sullivan got a hat-trick that day and I scored two tries.

Towards the end of the 1996 season, Saints came to Odsal and we murdered them 50–22. I scored in the first half and slightly showed the ball before scoring. I had been getting a bit of stick from Andy Northey. I liked him and we were good mates at Saints. He was known as 'The chest' – well, he called himself that. He was a funny lad and I enjoyed his company. Anyway, after I scored, he shoved me in the back and I ended up on the gravel race track. I had gravel marks on my hands and looked up to see Andy saying, "Don't take the mickey Loughlin".

It was always good playing against Saints because I had played with most of the players for years. Scott Gibbs got sent off in that Odsal match. I had been running riot past him before he got the red card. We used 'stand up' on him and exposed his lack of rugby league experience. Jon Scales and I had a field day running through gaps past him. I certainly wouldn't run straight at Gibbs as he would have put me over the stand. He just didn't have the awareness of an experienced rugby league centre; there is a big difference between playing centre in league and union.

They were hard games against Saints but usually entertaining and enterprising as they played the game the same way we did.

Bernard Dwyer
"I always wanted to do well playing against my old club. We had some big defeats against them, but we also had some big wins. Saints built on some young talent which matured at the time and they always seemed to beat us in finals. They were great days for Saints, then Bradford took some of the glory a few years later."

The week after the Saints match, Wigan came to Odsal and despite us going down to 12 men when Jeremy Donougher was sent off, we beat them too, 20–12. It was funny because prior to the back-to-back Saints and Wigan games I had been sent off in London for a high tackle. The disciplinary handed me a two-match ban which would have meant me missing both big games. I appealed and the decision was changed to sending off sufficient, but I had to pay a £500 fine. I paid it myself meaning I played in both games for nothing, but I wouldn't have missed them for the world.

I put Bernard in for a try against Wigan. It was a fantastic result as that Wigan side was a great team including Henry Paul, Jason Robinson, Andy Farrell and Gary Connolly. All those big names and we did them, that's how good the Bradford side was.

The Leeds games were hard but, to be honest, back then we used to smash Leeds off the park. With the exception of Adrian Morley, they weren't really up to scratch in the early years of Super League. There were some former Leeds lads in our side which helped spice things up a bit. There was a lot of feeling in the game and massive crowds. They were great to play in.

Brian Smith

"My first impressions of Paul were that he was a laid-back, laconic sort of bloke. He's a character that enjoys life. He had a very dry sense of humour and always had a line that could crack people up. As a player, I knew about him previously because he had played for Great Britain against Australia.

When Paul, Bernard and Sonny came to Bradford, I quickly learnt that Paul and Bernard were quite the double-act. With their humour, they were a big part in helping gel all the new players at Bradford together into a cohesive unit.

All the new players we brought to Bradford came within a few months of each other. The role that Lockers and Bernard had in bringing everyone together cannot be understated."

Lockers had a laconic sort of approach to training too. He was a cunning fox as he would always find a way to be third in line when it came to be picked to do something in training.

When I assisted Steve McNamara for the English tilt at the Four Nations in 2010, I was talking to some of the England squad about English players of the past and Lockers was one of the names that came up. My one regret would be that I only got to coach him for a short period of time."

My debut for Bradford. (Varley Picture Agency)

Back at Knowsley Road. Going past Keiron Cunningham for Bradford
Bulls during our 38–20 victory in July 1997. (Photo: Alex Service)

Brian Smith was an excellent coach; I wish I had learnt under him at the age of 16. He covered the basics of the game such as passing, but also how to look after yourself off the field. Although I had my good times off the pitch, I looked after myself through different types of training. That showed in the two seasons I had at Bradford. There was even talk of the RFL choosing me for the ill-fated Super League Great Britain tour in 1996. From what Bernard told me about it, and with players being sent home, I'm glad I didn't go.

Brian was very good on the video side of the game, analysing players' strengths and weaknesses and helping us understand the player we would be marking. I had never experienced that before. He was a top coach, proven by the number of players he signed who improved under him. He was a quiet bloke, very similar to his brother Tony. If I could have had someone like that to take me to one side when I was young and tell me when I wasn't putting enough effort in I'd have developed more quickly. When I started playing, the game seemed to be a lot more fun. In terms of dealing with players, Billy Benyon's strength was fitness and Alex Murphy's was team management. There wasn't any individual coaching as such back then. Eric Hughes and Clive Griffiths did all the coaching at the club. With Brian Smith, it was all about identifying what we were doing wrong and helping us improve.

Maybe if I'd had a coach like Brian back at the start of my career, I might not have had so many good times off the field. I saw some players who never relaxed, did too much training and it would lead to injuries and in some cases a shorter career. There's got to be a happy medium. It was easier to learn skills towards the end of my career because we were in full-time training.

In the 1980s it had been on a Tuesday night being flogged in the mud and freezing cold when nobody really wanted to be there. Thursday night would be a game of touch-and-pass, a run through the moves then straight to the Woodies pub. On Saturday morning we would sweat out the beer. There were no one-on-one skills sessions when the game was still part-time.

Bernard also wished he had received more Brian Smith-style coaching earlier in his career too. Brian made Bernard a more skilful player. He had always had skills, but Brian helped him learn more about his game and it took him to Great Britain recognition. I thought that Saints had 1950s and 1960s-style training when I was there.

There was 'trotting', scissor kicks on the floor, press ups and medicine balls on your stomach. It was like National Service.

Paddy Loughlin
"Paul never really pushed himself early in his career. Brian Smith would have taken him further earlier on."

At Bradford we had this machine we used to run through that had rubber bands on it. Due to my height, the rubber bands used to hit me in the testicles. No wonder Brian always thought I was third in the queue at training.

Bradford used to take us to Ampleforth on a pre-season training camp. It was like an old boarding school near York. It was in the middle of nowhere, 10 sharing a room and five miles to the nearest pub. We eventually made it to the pub one day and getting back to our digs, Bernard and I decided to have a sneaky fag. Little did we realise we were blowing smoke through Brian Smith's room window. We heard his Australian yell, "Who's fucking smoking?" I shouted, "It's Bernard" followed by a desperate shout of, "It's Lockers!" He must have thought "those two again".

Matty Elliott had been assistant to Brian and was of the same mould when he took over in 1997. Then 'Nobby', Brian Noble, was his assistant and continued in the same vein. It worked. Each coach brought their own little things in, but didn't change too much with the side. Ultimately, your favourite coach is the one who picks you.

I do have to say though that the skills I learnt at Bradford under Brian Smith and Matthew Elliott were incredible. It was all about going back to basics, catching and running good lines.

We had a big side and were very hard to beat in 1997 despite slipping up to Saints at Wembley. We ended up clinching the league at Sheffield with several weeks of the season still to play. The back line was massive. At full-back, there was Stuart Spruce. Then there was Abi Ekoku, Graham Bradley, myself, Matt Calland and Jon Scales. Then there was the huge pack, I think Bernard was the smallest player in the pack, but was still the hardest tackler.

Things didn't always go smoothly at Bradford. After a club day out at York Races we had a Yorkshire versus Lancashire 'toy fight' in a pub which got out of hand. It started off as messing around, and then it started getting serious. Little punches started getting thrown and it was off. The pub ended up getting wrecked and we had to pay for all the damage. We were all covered in blood as we got on the coach to get back to Bradford. Matt Elliott found out about the incident and when we played Warrington the week after, Brian McDermott and I were dropped to the bench as we looked the worst.

I had been so close to winning the league during my time at Saints but we'd never quite got there, then there were the Wembley finals we had lost. I had only won the Premiership and the John Player Special Trophy. I had not been used to tasting champagne so much. We won the 1997 Super League at Sheffield on a Saturday afternoon. We had to win the game to win the league. It was a tight pitch as always at the Don Valley. It seemed as if they had brought the touchlines a bit more than normal because I've never played on such a narrow pitch. It was a red- hot day and was packed, due to the Bulls fans who had made the trip. We knew it was going to be hard as a visit to Sheffield is always a physical game against their big forwards.

I think it was only 8–2 at half time. Matt Elliott got us into a big huddle and was telling us what we could do, that we could make history for the Bradford Bulls and make a bit of history for ourselves. He finished it by saying, "Remember Churchill's famous two words" and he walked out.

All the lads were really geed up by this, slapping each other in the chest. Big Paul Anderson was slapping Bernard, McDermott was cracking Bradley, and I spotted the seven-year-old ball boy, weighed him up and give him a crack...

We went down the tunnel waiting to get back on for the second half and I was still thinking about these two famous words that Churchill had said. I couldn't remember what they had been so decided to ask Bernard what they were. He turned round, looked at me and said, "Oh yes". Somehow, I don't think Matt Elliott had Churchill the insurance company dog in mind when he had been giving us the talk.

We won the game 32–12, and won the league. At last I had won something big in my career. Unfortunately, it wasn't with Saints, but winning the Super League with Bradford was the proudest achievement of my domestic career. It was a great feeling. After the game, Bernard, Simon Knox, Sonny and I went round St Helens town centre to celebrate. But the game had been so hot and hard that the friends we met couldn't believe that we weren't really knocking the drinks back. We were shattered and after a few drinks, we went home. The next day, we made up for it and really savoured it all. It didn't make up for all the near misses I'd had, but nobody can take it off me.

Bernard Dwyer

"Winning the league in 1997 was the icing on the cake. Bradford were destined to do well because of the people they had on board. There were Stuart Spruce, James Lowes and Steve McNamara just to name three. We knew they had big ambitions. The year before, Brian Smith had invited us into individual meetings. He asked me what I wanted to get out of the season and I told him I was hoping we would upset quite a few teams. He turned round and said to me, "We're going to win it this year." I looked at him and wondered if he had gone mad. The conviction in his face as he told me, "We'll win it this year and if we don't, we'll definitely win it next year," told its own story. I could tell he was serious. As history shows, we did well that first season but were head and shoulders above the rest the year after. It was a great end to the two years I had with Lockers at the club.

I can't speak highly enough of Bradford; they just gave us a second chance really. Not just Lockers and me, but some other players who had been discarded by clubs. It was all based around hard work but we had a great time at the club too. That was the start of Bradford's success."

There were a few games left and we went off the boil a bit. We were presented with the Super League trophy after the last game of the season which was an evening match at Odsal. The club set up a stage which the whole squad climbed onto. Robbie Paul lifted the trophy. We had done really well, the new side that had been assembled had got to Wembley and finished third in 1996 then returned to Wembley and blitzed the Super League in 1997. We even did OK in the 1997 World Club Challenge on the home leg but, like many English teams, we struggled on the other side of the world. There was a big gulf in class between us and the Australian sides.

With regard to the 1997 World Club Challenge away matches, I think all English clubs were the same. We went out there to give it a good go. We played Auckland first and started well by scoring. They just hammered us from that point. While we were out there, once we had trained, there wasn't much to do so most of us would end up going out for a drink. It was then over to our hotel in Sydney. We used to go down to one of the RSL clubs where they had indoor bowls. We were throwing schooners down like pop while playing darts. We didn't realise that the schooners are stronger alcohol than back home and all of a sudden we were flying. We would be playing skittles with old ladies in white suits. We were all over the place staggering. I think we got banned in the end. Then we'd go to the Hog's Breath cafes for steaks and burgers. I must have spent thousands over there on food and ale. The games and training got in the way of the holiday.

Bernard Dwyer

"We went away with Bradford in 1997 for the World Club Challenge. Paul was big on 'Shakespeares' while we were there. Paul had an injury at the time, he was struggling for fitness and he wasn't sure he was going to get picked. We had a couple of weeks in Auckland and there was a pub called The Shakespeare just down the road from our hotel. I didn't like drinking in the lead-up to a game and I was certain to play. He would just say to me, "I'm just going for a couple of Shakespeares" and would disappear for a couple of hours. Same again a few hours later. "Shakespeares" got a few mentions in our hotel at the time.

A couple of us were left out of the second game against Penrith. So I went out with Jeff Wittenberg, our big prop. He had some mates around there and I was invited out with them. At 10 o'clock, I had no idea where I was, we were really throwing them back. We ended up in this nightclub and I was dancing away. Jeff then told me we had to get back to the hotel. On the way back, we passed two minibuses at the side of the road that were used to take us to training. Jeff said, "Let the tyres down, it will give us another half an hour's rest." So, that's we did. I woke up in the morning, thinking "Oh no, what have I done?" The call went out to the squad that training was delayed while they got the tyres blown up. I told Bernard what we had done and not to tell anybody, but he just laughed.

The final game was against Cronulla and it was the game where I pulled off the best tackle of my career. It was against the Australian test prop Jason Stevens. He came onto a short ball and in an instinctive reaction I hit him with my shoulder and just dropped him flat. Even the Cronulla players came over to me and said, "Good hit mate". I was thinking I wish I could have done this earlier in my career. Graham Bradley scored two tries for us, but we still went on to get hammered. The party was then over. The three weeks came to an end and it had been a good bonding session. I'm sure other English clubs were the same.

Even though we hadn't won a game, due to the structure of the competition we ended up in the quarter-finals, playing Auckland in New Zealand. I was in the last couple of weeks of my contract and didn't go; I was at home sorting out a deal to join a new club. I had an option to stay at Bradford, but when I saw what they were offering me; I thought I could have made working down the launderette. Needless to say, Bradford got hammered by Auckland again, 62–14.

Bernard Dwyer

"Bradford embraced the Super League better than any other club. Paul was only there two years but we had two great years together there. It was a great place to be and exciting times for the club."

It's a shame to see Bradford struggle these days. The squad isn't as strong and the crowd has dipped. I played there in a community match recently for Ikram Butt. I got a good reception, but there wasn't the same buzz as there used to be. I'd got used to playing there in front of crowds of 20,000 on a regular basis. The lack of a crowd in a ground of that size is really noticeable.

Bradford put me into their Hall of Fame which was nice; there can't be too many people who are in the Bradford and St Helens Halls of Fames. Bernard also achieved this.

Wembley here we come! After beating Leigh at Central Park in the Challenge Cup semi-final in 1987. (Courtesy *St Helens Reporter*)

A team group for the season of my first Wembley Final: St Helens RLFC 1986-87. (Courtesy Alex Service)

8. Wembley finals

In 1987, St Helens played Leigh at Central Park in the semi-final for the right to play in the Challenge Cup Final at Wembley. Everybody was tipping us as strong favourites to beat them. It turned out to be a very close game though; Leigh had a number of St Helens lads in their side who left nothing out on the pitch. Barrie Ledger pulled off an incredible, late, last ditch tackle on John Henderson to prevent him from scoring. Barrie shot across the pitch diagonally to catch him and that tackle took him – and us – to Wembley. To reach Wembley was the fulfilment of a boyhood dream. I still have the picture on my wall of all the players and Alex celebrating after the semi. All the players had their shirts off and were clutching cans. It's a cracking picture.

Before Wembley in 1987, we recorded a song *The Saints go marching on* which featured lyrics like "We've got the greatest chairman, Lawrie Prescott is his name". Football teams had always made records when they made it to Wembley and we followed suit. A Saints fan had a recording studio in Liverpool and we went along to make the record. It was embarrassing really. We practised the song at the studio and none of us could sing. The chorus was a mess because we all kept jumping in at different times and in different keys. The studio owner got fed up in the end. Neil Holding then decided to keep messing it up on purpose. It should have taken us two hours to record, it ended up taking five.

We ended up publicising it, including a live appearance on the *Tom O' Connor Roadshow* on television. We were all wearing silver tracksuits with a white vee like the pop group Five Star. It was in fashion back then, all of us had moustaches too. Tom O'Connor was talking to Neil Holding before the show went live and ran through what he wanted to do. Tom said he was going to say that the team was here because we were preparing for Wembley and that we were going to train on the beach because Tom had heard that Red Rum had done the same thing; it was good for our legs and might give us the edge to win because Red Rum was a winner. Tom just wanted Neil to reply that we had been training. The show came on live and Tom introduced us as the Saints and said to Neil Holding that he believed we had been in Blackpool. Before Tom could give us his pep talk, Neil recited it back to him word-for-word to a stunned and stammering O' Connor. All the lads were laughing their heads off.

97

Richard Digance, the guitarist and singer, was also on the show and he was singing *A nightingale sang in Berkeley Square*. The chorus involved whistling which we also had to do. It was embarrassing especially when I saw one player trying to whistle with no teeth. Then there was me with my lisp and big teeth.

Our record must have sold about six copies, it was that good. My mum still has it at home, though.

Wigan and Widnes had not made it to Wembley, so we were tipped to lift the cup although Halifax had been doing well. In the run-up to the final, nobody wanted to get injured. It's a fair gap between the semi and the final, but we just had to put it to the back of our minds. Our form dipped a little - we were all focused on Wembley because none of our players had played there. We were all aware that a Wembley Challenge Cup Final might only happen once in a career. I've been fortunate to play there five times; there have been many players better than me who never made it there once. John Woods is just one example.

Part of the trouble I believe for Saints with those appearances at Wembley was that we would go down for a week. The players are allowed a couple of drinks so you know what that ends up like. The club would take us to the races. We would get bored and end up going for a pint. A week was too long.

Barrie Ledger

"I remember for Wembley in 1987 where we were in camp at the hotel. We should have all been in bed but a few of us were up and running about at daft o' clock. Alex Murphy had sent Dave Chisnall out to find out what was going on; someone must have reported us. Dave went round checking the rooms so we got back to our rooms as soon as we could. When he went into Paul's room, he found Paul sat in bed with a pair of shades on, smoking a cigarette with the porn channel on. He and Kevin McCormack were in the room next to me.

Alex pulled us all in the morning about it and said if he found out who had gone AWOL during the night, they wouldn't be playing in the Cup Final on the Saturday. Paul was man enough to own up and told Murphy he had been one of the people out."

The players arrived in the massive Wembley dressing room, the kit man had been there earlier and we saw our shirts hanging up in front of us. We started to get changed and engaged in jokey banter to try and relieve our nerves. All we were thinking about was the big game to come. Off in a corner, someone was being sick. There was a telly in the dressing room so we could see all the build up. Then there was the shout "five minutes". The two teams lined up together in the tunnel. While we were there, the crowd sang *Abide with me* and if that didn't bring tears to a player's eyes, there was something wrong with him. The hairs on the back of our necks were standing up while we were waiting in the tunnel. Then we walked out onto the pitch and took a look round. It was a deafening roar at first but then it tapered off.

The game went so quickly it's untrue. People told me that before my first Wembley but I didn't realise myself how quick it was until I had played in one.

Prince Phillip was the guest of honour in 1987. He came to me, took a look down and said, "You've got big feet haven't you?" I didn't really know what to say to that.

Wilf George got a controversial opening try for Halifax. He went past me and Tony Burke then Phil Veivers. I've never seen legs like that like those on Wilf George. He was a massive bloke to have on the wing. He was definitely in touch for that try. If there had been the video referee system back then, it wouldn't have been given. It was just one of those things.

Seamus McCallion scored another for them and we went in at half time 12–2 down. We scored shortly after the break with Mark Elia going 80 metres and rounding Graham Eadie. Elia was world class and for me, that was one of the best ever tries at Wembley. I kicked the goal. I owe a lot to Mark Elia who taught me how to run good lines. He told me not to run at the player, but at the gap, he was also a good passer of the ball.

The one thing we didn't do that day was get the ball wide enough. They had a big pack and we should never have got sucked into playing them down the middle of the park. Once we got the ball wide, we proved what we could do.

We made a change before a scrum with Paul Round coming on for Roy Haggerty. Halifax's John Pendlebury peeled away and sent in Graham Eadie. It was like in football when they say you should never make a substitution while waiting for a corner to be taken when you're defending.

We started to get on top a bit then because they were fading. I scored from a scrum. People ask how Saints have always played with a lot of flair, no matter the players on the field. I think it has something to do with always having class half-backs. When I was playing, there was Neil Holding who could pass both ways and Harry Pinner who was a ball-handling loose-forward. Then there were Brett Clark, Shane Cooper and Tommy Frodsham. I used to love playing with Tommy because he put me through gaps.

It was from running at a gap that I scored that try at Wembley in 1987. Mark went across, he gave it to me and I ran for the gap. I had been joking with Barrie Ledger the night before the final; we had been doing the walkabout on the Wembley pitch. I told Barrie, "I will get the ball here, run for the gap, Wilf George will come across to cover and I will give it to you for you to score in the corner." On the day itself, I dummied and scored myself.

The try at Wembley also meant I was part of the opening sequence of BBC Television's Saturday afternoon sports programme *Grandstand* every Saturday for a year, so if anyone would like 52 Betamax copies of the opening of *Grandstand* that year, let me know because my mum taped it every week.

I was still buzzing after that try when I went to take the conversion. I wasn't 100 per cent focused on the kick. I missed it. Paul Round scored another try. This time I kicked the goal to bring the score to 19–18 to Halifax.

We thought we had clinched the game when famously Mark Elia went over in the corner, but John Pendlebury knocked the ball out of his grasp. We then had another try disallowed for a forward pass.

People ask why we never went for a drop-goal, but we were so much on top, we thought we could score at any time. Players don't realise exactly how much time has passed in the game.

It was devastating. Everyone was upset, especially Chris Arkwright, our captain. Seeing hard players upset shows how devastating a Wembley loss is. I've experienced it five times. Some people say it is worse to lose in a semi-final than a final, but I totally disagree.

Chris Arkwright was recently inducted into the St Helens RLFC Hall Of Fame and, because he was captain of the 1987 Wembley side, he was asked about that game at the induction event. He said there was no way he was going to blame Mark Elia for what happened. I

On the attack against Halifax at Wembley 1987.

Scoring at Wembley in 1987. (Courtesy *St Helens Reporter*)

would never blame him either, if he had won us the game he would have won the Lance Todd Trophy.

There was a dinner in the hotel after the game with wives and girlfriends, the whole club was there. There was a disco and a few drinks. We travelled back the next day to St Helens Town Hall for a public reception. When we went back to the steps of the town hall, I grabbed the microphone and said, "To all the spoonheads, hang loose," which caused some puzzled looks among the crowd. Basically, Deano, who I have known for years, had a motorbike club of about 30 members. They were rockers really and went by the name of The Ashton-In-Makerfield Spoonyeds. I used to knock about with them and thought I would give them a shout at the Town Hall. I was made an honorary member and given a badge and a leather jacket.

There were quite a few supporters at the Town Hall in 1987, it would be a different story the next time we came back from Wembley.

To cap the misery, I injured my knee ligaments against Warrington after the 1987 Challenge Cup Final. That injury put me out for the entire pre-season for 1987–88.

Les Quirk saw us through to Wembley in 1989 with a late try against the much-fancied Widnes team in the semi-final at Central Park. Wigan and Widnes were the two big sides at this time. It was a brilliant win, 16–14, and a top game. They had beaten us at Wigan earlier in the season in the John Player Special Trophy semi-final by two points so it was a big confidence boost for us. However, to be fair Richard Eyres was sent off for a trip on Neil Holding. Les's try against Widnes in the semi-final is well remembered by Saints fans. Paul Groves, who was one of the most underrated players Saints have had, broke through showing Neil Holding-like pace, gave me the ball and I put Les in at the corner. He scored despite having three defenders around him.

Widnes were a quality side including Alan Tait, John Devereux, Jonathan Davies, Martin Offiah and a massive pack with Joe Grima, Phil McKenzie and Kurt Sorenson. At half-back was Tony Myler, one of the best players ever in that position, although he struggled with injury. For some reason though, we had a good record against them even beating them 25–0 at Knowsley Road at New Year in 1988.

One of the problems for St Helens at Wembley that year was that the two Australian players we had signed for short spells, Paul Vautin and Michael O'Connor, were flown back for the final. This meant local players were left out of the side and it caused some bad feeling. The decision about Vautin was understandable because he had had a good season with us. O'Connor had never settled in though and hadn't been outstanding, despite the high level he had played at in Australia. The lads left out were gutted, although they probably changed their minds when they saw the final itself.

A 17-year-old Gary Connolly was selected at full-back for the final and I believe one of the Wigan stars said some things to unsettle him in the tunnel before the game. It was just to get inside his head. It must have been tough for Gary that day. I've played full-back and it's one of those positions where if your side is doing well, a full-back can receive the ball in attack and it's the best position in the world. But if their side is struggling, the full-back can be on their own at the back and they need a baseball bat to stop people coming through. I don't think the game knocked Gary's confidence though because there was nothing he could have done. Even in his pomp, if he'd have played full-back in that game he wouldn't have changed much.

Two weeks before the final, I had gone on a run to my mum's. Coming up her steps, I slipped and cracked a bone in my ankle. By the time I got home, my ankle was like a balloon. I missed the league game against Halifax and had to have painkilling injections. The ankle was then strapped up; there was no way I should have played at Wembley really. It was a game I didn't want to miss though and I ended up playing with Dave Cosgrove's high boot on alongside one of my normal boots.

I ended up going off in the second half. Wigan hammered us; we were no match for them that day. They just tore us apart from the off. Kevin Iro went past me, Tony Burke and Phil Veivers to score after just three minutes and the writing was on the wall.

Before half time, we had a chance to kick a penalty so we wouldn't have been nilled, but we didn't go for it, we went for touch instead.

The second half was men against boys, 27–0 at the end. It was horrible, especially against Wigan. I remember coming back to St Helens on the coach and people were on the streets booing us. I felt like getting off the coach and booing myself. We all got drunk coming back, we were embarrassed. Saints will never live that one down.

It was a different feeling to 1987 because in the Halifax game, we knew we should have won, but time ran out on us. In 1989 we had just been trounced by one of the best sides of all time. They had laid the foundations for a great team. They were all internationals and if a player left, Wigan simply replaced them with another international. The Wigan side that defeated us 27–0 at Wembley would have given the Australian test side a run for their money.

After the game, if Alex Murphy had asked us "Who deserved to be here?" a hand wouldn't have gone up. The only possible exception was Neil Holding; he got St Helens man-of-the-match that day. In fact, it won him a holiday for two to New York. I believe the fans were hoping we would all win the prize and not return.

In 1991, Widnes were again our semi-final opponents at Central Park and again were tipped to beat us. However, we beat them convincingly 19–2. Wigan's new stand was being built at the time and I remember that some of our squad players stood on the steps of it to watch the game. Our confidence was high. We had started to play some good rugby and Mike McClennan was building a decent squad. Jonathan Griffiths was playing well, Alan Hunte was flying and Paul Bishop was pulling all the strings at scrum-half.

Before the final, Wigan had to play a number of fixtures in a short space of time to clear a backlog of matches. They had a few injuries and there was a feeling that we might be playing them at the right time. Denis Betts was struggling with his hamstring; Ellery Hanley had a fitness test on the pitch shortly before kick-off. It was hot as well.

Jon Neill tackled Andy Platt shortly after kick-off and split his ear open. I was glad it wasn't me – two big solid men clashing and bashing into each other.

I remember missing touch with a penalty kick; they knocked the ball back and scored. It was a schoolboy error on my part. We had been getting on top and that try knocked the stuffing out of us.

Just before half-time, Bernard Dwyer made a break. Les Quirk was one side of him, I was the other. If he'd have popped it to Les he'd have been in, but he went for it himself. On that Wembley pitch a player will see those posts and want to score himself.

Shortly after that, I went to tackle Steve Hampson. We clashed heads and I couldn't see properly because I ended up with double vision. I had to come off and a substituted player couldn't return. My final was finished. Phil Veivers also went off. The second half just passed me by. My vision came back to normal after about 20 minutes.

Alan Hunte scored for us and Paul Bishop kicked the goal from the touchline. We were giving them as good as we got but the game finished 13–8 to Wigan. It was disappointing to lose again and that was my last Wembley final with Saints.

In 1996, Bradford Bulls made it to the semi-final to play Leeds. First of all, I have to say as a St Helens lad there is nothing like a Saints versus Wigan game. However, Bradford versus Leeds is quite intense. We played the derby one year in front of nearly 24,000; I think it was a Super League record at the time. I scored in the semi-final and in the second half, made a break, drew the full-back and sent in 'Deadly' Paul Medley for a try. So, we get to the final and who do we play? Saints! I couldn't believe it.

I thought a lot of Brian Smith's decision to play Jon Hamer at Wembley in 1996 despite Hamer not becoming a full-time player because he was a policeman. All the other players were now full-time, and most part-time players had dropped out of Super League.

Saints were red-hot favourites for the final. However, we played some really good rugby and we took a huge 26–12 lead in the second half. Robbie Paul scored a hat-trick, Bernard got over for his Wembley try. I remember Graham Bradley had lost at Wembley with Castleford in 1993 and at 26–12 he walked up to me and said, "We'll get our winners' medals now." I thought "Don't speak too soon." Then came Bobbie Goulding's bombs. Everybody blames our full-back Nathan Graham, but he only spilled a couple. If they had had the video referee for the Cup that year, it would have shown Saints' players offside, plus obstruction and a knock-on for a couple of those three tries from kicks. The game went away from us. I went to full-back in place of Graham. I couldn't believe how close we had been. Apollo Perelini ran over me for the final try. He came in off a short ball and there was no stopping him. The whole Bradford team wouldn't have stopped him.

I remember seeing Phil Veivers at full-time. He had played in every round for Saints leading up to the final, then had been left out for Wembley. He put his arm round my shoulder and I told him: "Don't look at him getting that fucking cup" as Goulding went to lift the trophy. Phil's situation was probably worse than losing at Wembley. Seeing his side win but not being involved, especially after all the years he had been at the club, must have been tough. He had lost at Wembley three times before and it must have been sickening for him to miss out on their victory. I think they gave him a medal, but I think he gave it to his lad in the end. It must have been traumatic for Phil.

Bradford Bulls before the 1996 Challenge Cup Final.

Bernard and I had spent so long at Saints. For us to leave and then, the very next season, lose to them at Wembley was hard to take. It seemed a bit unfair. There were some lads in that Saints team who hadn't been there two minutes and didn't stay at the club much longer who were walking round with winners' medals.

I'm not bitter and twisted, well maybe a little... It was a horrible day for me, Phil and Bernard. That some people say it was the greatest Wembley final of all time is little consolation. It was great for supporters, but not for players on the losing side. It's certainly not the best game I've ever played in.

Robbie Paul got £10,000 for that first Wembley hat-trick. With smaller prizes, the players put money into a team kitty. However, with a bigger award, the player kept it. All the man-of-the-match awards and so on were pooled and spent on the end-of-season team holiday.

We had our chance again against Saints the year after and this time Bradford started favourites after another victory over Leeds in the semi-final. We hadn't been beaten so far that season while heading to Wembley. The club introduced skin-tight yellow jerseys for us to wear in the final. It took a couple of days to get Bernard's off. The tops didn't suit him, Paul Anderson and Paul Medley. They were fine for the slim lads like me! It was the skin-tight shorts that used to do Bernard; they made him look like Dafydd from television's *Little Britain*.

One should never underestimate Saints, but we were very confident in 1997 that we would win. We were flying high at the top of

Super League, but Saints just did us again on the day. We were expecting big kicks, but they were putting little grubbers in.

Both sides swapped tries in the early stages of the final then I scored an interception to give us a 10–4 lead. The interception was off Karle Hammond. Now, Karle was a good player, but I remember looking at him early in the game. For me he embodied the players who had been at Saints for just a short period and won trophies. From a scrum, he got the ball and I clattered him, breaking his nose. The referee called me over saying, "If that had been near the end I'd have sent you off". Fortunately for me, this was in the first five minutes. The next time, Karle got the ball he must have been looking for me coming at him, because he made a pass that I plucked out of the air and scored under the sticks. I scored a try in every round of the Cup that year. We had a brilliant team that year. However, Robbie Paul had struggled with a broken foot and took a knock during the game. At the end of the day we lost 32–22.

That was my last Wembley final, five losers' medals. I say to Bernard that with his four and my five, we could melt them and make our own cup. Bernard did get a winners' medal with Bradford after I left.

The cover of the cassette single that St Helens released in 1987 when we
reached Wembley. Sadly, my show business career did not take off.
(Courtesy Alex Service)

9. Huddersfield

When I left Bradford, I trained with Andy Gregory's Salford. I was going to sign for them, but sadly Bradford were a little bit petty I thought, and wanted £7,000 to let me go. They had had two good years out of me and I was soon to be 32 years old. I thought they should have let me go for nothing. Salford were willing to make me a good contract offer for two years but weren't prepared to pay a transfer fee.

Phil was at Huddersfield at this time; Garry Schofield was coach and had just got them promoted. I was playing darts with Phil on a Monday night and he asked me to sign for them. All the lads in the pub used to take the mickey out of Phil saying he was always pleading with me to join him there. Phil was assistant coach and he spoke to Garry about me. Garry told him to tell me that they would match what Salford had offered me. I asked for a car as well which they gave me – I thought that if I could get two years out of it, that would be great. I signed for them and used to travel from St Helens with Phil.

I was made up to be at Huddersfield, it was a massive stadium with lovely facilities. I knew some of the players there. Two of the older blokes behind the scenes at the club had played against my dad. The kitman was good and so on. It was a shame that the team couldn't match the facilities.

I had only been there four months when, in July 1998, Schofield had to leave due to his lack of coaching badges. Phil took over then and my first question was if I could still travel over with him. People ask me if it was awkward to be coached by a mate when I was with Phil Veivers at Huddersfield. It was funny really because, on a Sunday night after a game, Phil and I used to go out with a few lads from a local labour club for a drink. The next morning, we'd head into training a little hung over. We would stop half a mile away from the training ground at a little general store we had found and buy a clove of garlic. We'd eat that to get rid of the beer fumes. All the lads at training would be complaining about my breath, asking if I had been to a curry house the night before. But now he was our new head coach and I was with him.

Phil used to go over the top with me a little bit in training sessions; he probably thought that if he didn't get on my back the other lads would think he was favouring his mate. Then, when back in the car, he would apologise and say that was just the way it had to be. Phil will make a good coach one day, I am sure of that. He was unfortunate back then because he had new ideas, but Huddersfield didn't have much money for new players at the time. I thought his training sessions were better than Schoey's.

John Bentley was with Huddersfield at the same time as me. He was a real character and a fitness fanatic. He had come back to league from rugby union and did all right for Huddersfield. He had a gift for getting the players going at training, but was able to do it with a smile. At the club they had a gym with a sunbed. I used to go on it. One day I was lying on the sunbed, the next thing the cover was flung open and a big nettle bush was hurled onto me by John Bentley. I flew off the sunbed, all red with lumps all over me. I never went on it again.

Ken Davy was the chairman and he put a lot of money into getting the club into Super League. There were some players there on what I thought was very high money. When they were in the First Division, the game's second tier, they had players who were earning more money than some of their counterparts in Super League. They got promoted and they needed to invest in new players, but they didn't. It's happened for them now though, I think Phil and I turned it round just like Bernard and I did at Bradford. Everywhere I leave, success is just around the corner. Mal Reilly ended up taking over at Huddersfield at the end of August, and I left in 1999, towards the end of his first full season in charge.

I broke my left arm while at Huddersfield. The break was just unfortunate, I went to tackle Richie Blackmore, the Leeds centre, but I hit the top of his head with my arm. He had earlier thrown the ball at me for what he thought was a high tackle, so I thought the next time he ran at me I would let him have it, but it didn't work out well for me.

Phil had put himself on the bench and had to come on for me. He dived for a loose ball and Francis Cummins's knee just happened to catch him in the side of his head. Phil's head came up like something from a cartoon. They tried to drain it in the dressing room later, but it wouldn't go down. They bandaged it all up and gave him painkillers. He had driven me to the game, but was now all groggy so was insisting I drove home. I asked him if he was having a laugh because I had a broken arm. Phil managed to get us back and, on the way, I rang up my local club and ordered us eight pints of Guinness because we would only get there around 11pm. We walked in to a stunned silence with our pints waiting for us on the bar. Phil had his head wrapped up like a mummy and I had a broken arm.

Someone asked me recently what happened to Sonny, Bernard and me when we left Bradford. I explained that we had all enjoyed a bit of success. Sonny returned to Saints where he won a Grand Final and a World Club Challenge. Bernard won the Challenge Cup Final with Bradford and went on to join the coaching staff. Meanwhile, I went to Huddersfield and won about six games in two years... It all turned out well for us.

It was hard when we had days like the one when we came to Knowsley Road in 1998 and lost 68–18. That was embarrassing. We just weren't strong enough; it wasn't for the lack of effort. As well as Phil, Bobbie and me, Danny Arnold, Jon Neill and Ian Pickavance, who signed in 1999, made up the former Saints contingent at the McAlpine. Basil Richards and Joe Berry were two good forwards as was Neil Harmon. Then there was one of Super League's best hookers in Danny Russell. We needed about five quality players to take us to the next level. However, at 33, I was on my last legs.

Phil had got all his coaching badges, but I think Huddersfield just wanted a high-profile coach to replace Schofield. Mal Reilly had been Great Britain coach so he was a good catch for the club, but ultimately, he didn't have enough to work with. He tried his best and brought a couple of players from Newcastle, where he had been coaching in Australia, but they were only reserve graders. We had no depth in the squad and if we got injuries, we had to throw young lads in. It's hard blooding youngsters in a good team, let alone a struggling outfit. I enjoyed my time at the club, apart from the actual playing. The crowds were poor too; it felt like playing in the park at times.

Mal Reilly was ultra-competitive and there were many tales of him doing things like beating the rest of the Great Britain squad in a competition to see who could do the most lengths of the pool underwater without coming up for air. We did it at Huddersfield with him. We went over to Spain for a training week in January. We went to the pool and it felt like minus 10. They talk about mental toughness, but Mal Reilly is mental and tough. John Bentley and he were seeing who could do the most lengths and John ended up doing three lengths without coming up for air. Mal was purple when he came out of the water from trying to beat John and he only just failed. I just dipped my toe in and got out, saying, "You've won".

111

Mate against mate. Bernard Dwyer playing for Bradford Bulls ready to tackle me when I was with Huddersfield. (RL photos.com – Sig Kasatkin)

Kicking clear for Huddersfield, with Bobbie Goulding looking on.
(RL photos.com – Sig Kasatkin)

10. Swinton

I signed for Swinton when Mike Gregory was coaching there. I had left Huddersfield and got a job at Pilkingtons in St Helens. I was going to pack the rugby in. I bumped into Mike Gregory at Wickes DIY store in Wigan, of all places. He asked me what I was doing and when I told him I had packed in playing he said I should go and play part-time for him at Swinton. It was back to how I had started. Mike saw the chairman and they sorted me out with some money - not so much. I went down there and had a good season. Jon Neill and Ian Pickavance were with me again, and then later Phil joined too.

I remember my first training session for Swinton which took place at a local park. Paul Barrow took me there with Sean Casey from Haydock Island. It was like going back to the start of my career. It was a horrible, muddy pitch. I couldn't wait to get for it to be over to be honest. We later started training at Orrell which wasn't too bad.

But I enjoyed my time at Swinton. The first season was good. It was a noticeable step down from Super League though. My first game was at Workington, on Boxing Day 1999, the first match of the season. I played stand-off. I felt like Wally Lewis, I had so much time on the ball. There were some good players at Swinton though, including former Warrington winger Richard Henare, and former Saints loose-forward Sean Casey. Marlon Billy and Ian Watson were also there.

At that level, there were always opposition players who wanted to make a name for themselves at my expense and give me a bit of a crack. It's part of the game though and I had to expect it. I had tried to do it myself years earlier when Jonathan Davies had first moved to rugby league. I thought, "I'll show you, you rugby union so-and-so" and I couldn't catch him. He would sidestep me and I would end up waving to someone in the crowd.

We all used to take the mickey out of Mike Gregory's video sessions. Mike had a strong Wigan accent, but when he was talking us through the video session he would occasionally pronounce certain words in a strange 'posh' accent such as "keep your sha-ape". One day we went into for a video session after a game where we had been hammered at Workington. Mike announced, "You're all going to sit here and watch this game, nobody can move a muscle." Unbeknown to Mike, someone had swapped the match tape for porn. He shouldn't have been too annoyed though, whichever tape we watched we were going to see someone getting dicked. It broke the mood a bit because Mike had been fuming.

Mike was a good laugh, though. He had his mate there 'Chaddy' who was the conditioner and had previously been one of the trainers at Warrington. He could tell a tale. We played a match in Cumbria one day. Chaddy started telling a tale as we left Swinton and just about finished it when we arrived in Cumbria. He was a cracking bloke.

We played at Bury FC's Gigg Lane ground and with it being a football club, the facilities and the playing surface were nice. The food they put on after games was cracking; I used to bring my family for a meal. The pitch was like a carpet, but I think that worked against us as opposition teams enjoyed playing on it so much and looked forward to coming. It certainly made a change from places like Whitehaven or Batley where we played on the side of a hill.

I even got to play against Saints one last time in the Challenge Cup in 2000. I got on the score sheet kicking a goal. I took a bomb in the second half, sidestepped Apollo Perelini and saw Keiron Cunningham coming towards me. I went over on my ankle and cracked a bone in it. That was the end of my afternoon. We gave them a really good game that day though, and had been leading 16–10 at half-time. Sean Casey had a blinder and scored a good try. Those were the good times.

The downside was when we played Leeds in the Challenge Cup in 2001 and they scored more 106 points against us at Gigg Lane. Thinking about it, there can't be many professional rugby league players to have been on sides who have scored and conceded 100 points in separate games. Anyway, Tonie Carroll was playing at centre for Leeds that day and he didn't score so I did my job. I jokingly said that if they had all tackled like me, we would have won. I did score one of our tries as well.

People still remembered me in St Helens and it was nice to get recognised by people around the town. The strangest time I ever got recognised was during my spell at Swinton when I was working as a labourer in Manchester with a mate of mine called Jimmy Dixon. He was a cracking bloke who also used to go to the Old Road Labour Club too. We were having some butties on our dinner break one day when a Turkish fellow rode past on his bike, pointed at me and yelled, "Great player, great player". Jimmy asked me who he was and I told him I had no idea as we both burst out laughing. The next day, the same fellow came past again shouting, "Great player, you must come

114

in my kebab shop around the corner". I have no idea how this fellow knew me because he could hardly speak English. Jimmy must have thought I had set it all up because it became a talking point between us for months.

We eventually went into the shop and got free kebabs. Maybe he hadn't recognised me at all, Jimmy used to play bagatelle, maybe the fella had recognised him instead. Being honest though, outside of the game's heartlands, most rugby league players wouldn't get recognised back then.

Mike Gregory left to coach Wigan and Phil took over as Swinton coach. Phil brought my younger brother Michael to the club. My last professional rugby league game ever was a great memory because my younger brother Michael played alongside me for the one and only time. There is an age difference of 15 years between us. I had already retired really because it was getting to be too hard on my body, plus I knew if I got injured and couldn't work, that would make life very tough. It was the last game of the season against Dewsbury, on 1 July 2001, and they were short of players so they asked me if I could play. They were in the play-off places in the league and with Michael playing for Swinton, I said yes. Michael, my dad and I drove there with Phil Veivers. It was a proud day for the Loughlin family and my dad has the picture of the pair of us that day up on the wall of his pub. We won as well, 42–16.

It was a bit sad knowing that was my last ever game of professional rugby league, but at least I finished on a winning note. I only really reflected on it months later and it was all gone then. I started at 17 getting the bus from Ashton to Knowsley Road and finished it all off at Dewsbury for Swinton. Like I say, it was sad but I'd do it all again.

After that, I played a season of rugby union for Oldham. I didn't have to train and they gave me a few quid. After a full season, I had got the ball twice and kicked it twice. I didn't have to do any tackling, I could have played with my headphones on. I enjoyed the craic anyway. We were in the North Lancs & Cumbria League and used to have cans on the coach coming back - what a laugh. All the money they gave me for playing I ended up spending on ale.

Last appearance for Swinton, with my brother Mike and my dad.

Left: My brother Mike playing for Pilkington Recs.
(Photo: Alex Service)

11. On the groundstaff

I used to work on the groundstaff at Knowsley Road with Phil Veivers and Neil Holding. I was there for six years. They learnt that I have a fear of rats. I saw a rat once while walking my dog, it was massive. I checked behind me to make sure nobody was about then let out a scream. I hate them. There used to be loads of rats at Knowsley Road, because of the allotments at the back of the ground.

The groundstaff were always playing tricks on each other. At break time we used to take it in turns to make coffee. I'm a big coffee drinker and it was my turn to brew up. I took the lid off the coffee jar and there was a rat there. Neil and Phil were hiding behind the door giggling.

Neil used to take his Labrador Gemma to the ground, she ended up being pretty much part of the staff. He used to take her everywhere with him. One day, Shane, Phil Veivers and I were playing football at the side of the main stand using a set of red doors as the goal. Neil was going round the pitch, scooping up his dog's mess. He threw it over the fence, right onto Shane Cooper's head. Shane went mad, chasing Neil while Phil and I were on the floor laughing. Shane used to hate that dog.

Neil would tie a five pound note to a piece of string. We would hide behind the stone wall outside the ground on Knowsley Road and he would put the note on the pavement on the other side of the wall. He would wait till people tried to pick the note up then snatch it away. We were doing this one day when I noticed a policeman walking over the road. I warned Neil that a copper was coming. We were all giggling like little kids. Neil did the same thing with the copper.

If anyone sat with Neil Holding for five minutes, afterwards he would be able to impersonate them. I remember one of the kitmen at the club sadly died and we attended the funeral. When we worked on the ground, if somebody died at the club we would have to carry the coffin. We were all standing outside a church in Rainford waiting for the coffin to arrive. People were going past shaking our hands and so on. This old woman came past who had no front teeth. She said, "It's a bloody shame in't it." As soon as she had gone, Neil had popped his teeth out and did a spot-on impersonation of her. That was it, we were all gone. I was holding the laughter in as best as I could, but Phil was reduced to tears. One of the directors walked past and said: "Young Phil's taking it hard isn't he?"

Neil also once locked me in the toilets at the ground when I was painting. The toilets were underneath the stand. They used to say the toilets were haunted because a groundsman had committed suicide at the ground many years ago. So one Monday, I was painting the toilets. Neil had switched the lights off at the bottom of the stand and it was pitch black. I came out of the toilets and walked towards the little door at the back of the stand. I heard this door creak and looked at it; suddenly an old man's face partially obscured by a duffel coat came out at me. I took off; it was the fastest I ever moved at Knowsley Road. It had been Neil wearing a mask.

Neil Holding was murder. Before a game the kitman used to come round with a bottle of sherry. We'd have a little swig which we thought would open our airways. Neil would put his thumb over the top of the bottle and pretend to down the whole bottle. He'd then stagger round the dressing room acting drunk and slurring his words. The kitman was distraught, maybe he thought he would miss out.

There were some characters behind the scenes at Saints too. Monica used to clean all the kits. Neil Holding used to play tricks on her all the time. He would get a pair of undies then rub dry coffee in it to make it look like as if they were soiled. He'd run round chasing her with these trying to put them on her head. She was a lovely woman and worked really hard. All the lads would get her a bottle of Guinness at training.

Eric Edwards, the groundsman, would stop us training on the pitch, I'm sure he felt it belonged to the groundstaff. John the chef was another character, we used to train on a Saturday morning and he would do us a curry for lunch. The restaurant would be open for lunch every day and I'm sure on a Friday when he had finished, he would get all the leftovers and stick them in our Saturday curry. There would be bits of fish in it and chicken. We would ask him on Monday, "What's in our curry this week?" He would tell us to look at the menus and take our pick because it would all be in there come Saturday.

Neil Holding

"Paul was only a young lad when I first met him. He was a junior Saint and the first team had to go and meet them and answer their questions. His question was to ask me what colour underpants I wore.

118

Typical Lockers. Probably his mate had dared him to ask it; it's that long ago I can't even remember my answer.

Years later, we had seen him play in the colts. For his age, he was a big lad, but we felt he looked a bit raw at that point. All of a sudden, after a couple of games in the first team, he started to find his feet. His kicking ability was second to none, he was phenomenal. He just gelled with the rest of us. Because he's a local lad - and no disrespect to overseas players or those from outside the borough - I think he fitted in more. He was easy going and good for a laugh. He joined in all our conversations. Later, he used to work on the ground with me - I was the sheep and he was the sheepdog. Whenever I went, he followed behind. He wasn't a lover of work though, he would shirk, the lazy rat.

Because I lived near Paul at the time, we became very close. He would even call in for his tea after work. I used to have an open log fire and he would go in, take his shoes off, sit in my chair and fall asleep.

I used to take my golden Labrador to Saints with me. One day I left her at home and she escaped. Paul was driving back from Saints and stopped at some traffic lights. By some miracle, my dog was sitting there. He wound the window down, shouted to her, she jumped in the car and he took her home. The dog used to follow him round more than it used to follow me. Mind you, he was closer to the dog than he was to me.

The Duke of Edinburgh awards were being presented at Saints by Eunice Huthart who had won Gladiators on television. There was a kid in a wheelchair, Lockers said he would push him. I offered to help him but he insisted he would be fine. He pushed him down the old, narrow tunnel at Saints. By the time he got to the end of that short tunnel, it had taken him about two and a half minutes and he was sweating like hell. He asked me to get hold of the front wheels while he kept hold of the handles so we could lift him onto the turf. The second the wheels touched the ground, 'bzzz' the kid was off, it was an electric wheelchair. Lockers was swearing, I had to tell him: 'Paul, he's not deaf, he's just broken his leg.' If I tell the story with Paul present, he still gets embarrassed to this day.

I told him I could write his book for him because I have been in that many scrapes with him. Sky TV came once to interview him. My dog was following him while I was up on the main stand polishing the

119

floodlights. While I was up there, he shouted up to me: 'Mind you don't miss any, I think you've missed a spot up there,' as though he was my boss. I was effing and jeffing at him under my breath.

But despite all this there are lots of positive things I could say about Paul and really I have nothing negative to say about him at all.

I remember going on his stag do round Ashton. We'd both had a drink, but were telling each other we loved each other like two women watching Take That.

I'm pretty close to Lockers and he's godfather to my lads. He is a decent fellow."

12. Reflections

The first house I bought was in Garswood, shortly after I lost my driving licence. I thought I had been living at my mum's a bit too long and felt the property would be a good investment. I sold it, but still live in the same area today. We had some good parties in there; it's calmed down a bit now we have young kids. Once they grow up though and move on, the parties can start again. Millie's aged 9 and Tom is 13. Tom tried rugby, but it wasn't for him, he's now in the Wigan Theatre Company. He treads the boards and is a good actor. He does his own pantomimes for young school kids. I don't know where it comes from although one wag did say, "He'll never be as good an actor as his dad was." He taught himself to play the piano. He's a good looking lad too. He's nearly six foot already. It doesn't matter what my kids do for a living though as long as they're polite; they both are.

We love going to the Haven holiday site in Pwllheli. I used to love it there; we would go with Deano and his wife in caravans. We would drive round going to different beaches. It would be like going to Spain because the water was beautiful; there were porpoises in the water. I've seen a basking shark there too. We would spend red-hot days on the beach. I would come back from those holidays and people would notice the colour on me and wonder which far-flung travel destination I had visited. They were always surprised when I told them North Wales. People don't realise how beautiful it is and think of it in terms of places like Rhyl. We even had our honeymoon at Pwllheli.

On holiday with my family in Norfolk in 2011.

As for the favourite moments of my career, obviously signing for Saints was one of the biggest joys, then getting selected for the international set up. The biggest for me though was being inducted into the St Helens RLFC Hall Of Fame. That was my proudest moment.

My favourite game was either the 32–22 comeback at Central Park or the 'Coors' game in 1992. The tries I made at Saints that stand out are probably the couple of passes I gave to Les Quirk at Central Park that took us to Wembley in 1989. It was a very tight game against Widnes and Les got the winner.

Paddy Loughlin

"My favourite moments during Paul's career were when he was picked for test matches. The John Player Special Final against Leeds was another highlight; I've still got the video and the programme.

The biggest disappointments were, of course, the Wembley trips. I felt for him. He did something that players who had played for 15 or even 20 years didn't do and played at Wembley. There are many household rugby league names who never played there. Three out of the five finals his side should have won. I believe Saints should have beaten Halifax and Bradford should have beaten Saints both times.

However, he got a Championship medal and came back as player of the 1988 tour so there were some big plusses. I enjoyed watching him play although I can't say I enjoyed seeing him get hurt."

For the St Helens home game against Hull KR in 2010, they had a parade of the legends representing different eras in the club's history. For the 1980s there was me, Bernard Dwyer, Harry Pinner, Paul Forber, Neil Holding, Chris Arkwright and Barrie Ledger. Peter Gorley was there too and I hadn't seen him in years. When I made my debut, he was the first bloke I saw. He took his top off and was a huge, muscly bloke. I just wanted to put my shirt back on as quickly as possible because I didn't look great standing next to him. For the 1990s there was Alan Hunte and so on. There was also Dean Busby and I had no idea he still lived in St Helens, I assumed he had moved back to Hull. It was the first time I had seen him in around 15 years. The lap of honour was good; it was just great to see the players I had played with. There were also the older players like Dave Chisnall and everyone received a good reception from the crowd.

After the game, Phil took me straight home. A few players decided to have one last, naked run round the pitch in full view of everyone in the restaurant. They left their clothes to one side so Neil Holding kindly put the sprinklers on and soaked their clothes. They weren't too happy. I'm glad I didn't do it although I have done it before. It used to be done after training, a couple of laps in the 'knack'.

I did a sprint in the knack once. I was in the dressing room after training and had just had a shower. Les Quirk, who lived in the middle of nowhere, knew that neither Anthony Sullivan nor I liked mice. What Sully and I didn't know, but the rest of the lads did, was that Les had been spending time at home catching mice. He had put two mice in my bag. I pulled my towel out of my bag and a mouse landed on my knee as all the lads started sniggering. I jumped up, Anthony Sullivan screamed as the other mouse had jumped on his leg. We set off running and it's the only time I ever beat Anthony Sullivan for pace. We both powered out down the tunnel to the pitch naked.

Geoff Pimblett is the main organiser of the Past Players Association. Past players used to get a couple of free stand passes for each game, but apparently some people were abusing it and selling the tickets on. They changed it to issuing a ticket for the terraces at Knowsley Road unless you were of a certain age and needed a seat in the stand. When I left Saints and while my lad was only young, I wanted him to have a ticket for a game. They wanted eight quid for it and that annoyed me after all the years I had given them. It put me off going for a bit. I've been to a few games since, though.

The Past Players also organise a coach every year to the Grand Final which is something I go on. It's about £50 and we get a match ticket, a meal at Lancashire Cricket Club, cans on the coach and they do a drop-off near my house. It's so popular we pretty much have to book it once the hooter sounds at the previous Grand Final. It's a good day out and obviously better if Saints are there.

I used to love the Knowsley Road pitch. I used to know every blade of grass, especially as a goalkicker. I knew where to kick. Kicking goals seemed to be a lot easier at home, maybe at away games there were different pressures. It was always a brilliant pitch, that was down to the groundstaff such as Eric Edwards and Neil Holding. Eric would stop us training on it, it was his pride and joy. It has always suited Saints with the style of rugby the side has always played. The atmosphere was brilliant especially when it was full. With it being a big, open ground, if there wasn't a full house we could sometimes hear the individual comments of the supporters which could be funny.

It was the whole fabric of the place from the changing rooms onwards. After a game, we would all stay at the club together. It was a good feeling there. Saints will really miss it. It is sad that Knowsley Road is no more and it could affect the team. It affects players when they are away from their own ground and their own little routines. It's like playing away every week. It's going to be like starting again in many respects. But the new ground is for the better. They had to get one because Knowsley Road eventually didn't keep up with the team.

The facilities for players at Knowsley Road when I played were ancient. I don't think they had been changed since the ground had first opened. The bath used to be cracking though before health and safety regulations meant we all had to have showers. Everybody used to pile into that bath. If there had been a couple of arguments on the pitch, it could carry on in there although I never really saw that during my time at the club. I could imagine in the 1950s and 1960s problems would have been sorted out in that bath. We would sit in the bath with the water up to our necks; it would be full of mud and blood. One particular player, a good friend of mine, would also leave a little parcel as he was getting out of the bath that I would try and avoid as it floated past my face. The bath was the meeting place and even if a player hadn't trained, they would still get in the bath.

Even when we had physio on a Monday, we would still fill the bath up and get in. Wigan's Central Park was worse. They had two separate dressing rooms, but only one big bath for both sides. Players like Shaun Wane and Paul Forber would often have a set-to during the game and, although matters usually stayed on the field, it did mean there was considerable tension in the bath. Include the Saints and Wigan rivalry, and that is probably one of the reasons why they ended up stopping the practice.

I used to like Knowsley Road though. The walk down the dark tunnel to the pitch was a magic experience. As soon as we came out of it, the noise and light would hit us, it was brilliant. Even when we walked down it in 2010 for the Legends Parade, it made the hairs on the back of my neck stand up. We were swapping memories in the tunnel, although some players who have put on weight since their playing days struggled to fit down it.

124

It goes without saying that there were also numerous broken nose and rib injuries I suffered during my career. Rolling my ankle was always a painful injury. Nothing compares to the time I split my scrotum open though. We were playing Rochdale at home, there was a loose ball (ironically enough) that I dived on. Stuart Galbraith, their scrum-half stood on me although I thought it was their prop Neil Cowie. It was an accident, it split my shorts, I looked down and one of my balls was hanging out through the skin and through my jockstrap. There was no blood or anything. It looked like a golf ball hanging out. I was shouting to Cowie, "I'll kill you when I get hold of you". He told me it wasn't him. Jeanette came on; John Harrison had to look away and was smirking. I asked him what was up and he just told me not to look down. I couldn't get up in case my testicle fell out. They had to get a stretcher for me. A St Johns Ambulance man came on and for the sake of public decency placed his hat over the area concerned. I thought, "Oh yeah, tell the whole crowd." I went to Whiston Hospital and had microsurgery. They cleaned it out with cotton buds, and put some painkillers in. I had 12 stitches all the way around my balls. My dad came and was laughing. I still had my kit on. I had to wait an hour then I could go. I rang my mate Deano to get me a pint of Guinness and a cig. I had a shower then went to leave and someone had nicked my car keys and my wallet. They found my sponsored car in Huyton. I wasn't bothered about my car with it because it was a sponsored one, but that six quid in my wallet hurt.

I was also knocked out a couple of times. Once was at Swinton. I went down for a loose ball at the same time as Paul Topping went to kick it, he caught the back of my head instead. I woke up in the changing rooms with my dad next to me. As I was coming round, Arkie was waving tickets for his testimonial dinner under my nose saying, "So you wanted six tickets for my dinner then?"

Paddy Loughlin
"He had some bad knocks but he came back like the good 'un he was. He really frightened me at Swinton one time when he got knocked out and wasn't moving. I was trying to get into the dressing room, Joe Pickavance the Saints director got me let through. When I got in, Arkie was waving benefit tickets under his nose asking him how many did he want, five or 10? I felt better when I saw him do that because it was typical dressing room humour. Players never get any sympathy in the

dressing room when they get hurt. It wasn't as bad as we thought fortunately."

I had teeth knocked out too and it was horrible after when you had to push your gumshield back in onto your gums and nerves. It was against a Great Britain centre and at the start of the game I said, "Are we having it easy today?"

"Aye, alright", came the reply. Of course, it was light years away from being easy. We were both well over six feet and were cracking each other hard. He caught me in the second half and I lost teeth and had to have stitches inside my mouth.

Paddy Loughlin

"Paul's mum used to get very defensive while watching him play. If she heard a supporter criticising him, she would have her sleeves rolled up ready for battle! Once when Saints were playing Widnes, she was getting set to give Andy Currier some stick because he and Paul always used to have a dig at each other. I stopped her just in time to introduce her to Andy's dad who was sitting behind us."

All injuries tended to be more painful the day after the game. It was difficult getting out of bed sometimes when I was 25. It just got worse as I got older. I dread to think how hard it is for James Graham getting out of bed with the hammer he gets. At least they have full-time training and physios these days.

There were times when I would get out of bed the morning after a game to go on shifts at 5 o'clock. I would be stiff as a board, have a black eye, bruised ribs, sore knee and have a bit of a hangover. It wasn't much fun.

There was a machine we used to use for treating injuries at Saints. It had electrodes on it, used to stimulate our muscles. We would have the electrodes strapped to our legs, and then somebody would come in and switch the machine up to full power. The player would end up jittering as if they were sat on the electric chair - 'old sparky'. We would have acupuncture and be trying to relax when someone would come in and start jabbing the needles into our legs.

The most vocal fans apart from Saints fans were probably Wigan when they were in their pomp and getting huge crowds. And I used to like playing at Thrum Hall against Halifax. It was a tight ground with the supporters close to the pitch. The crowd would never be massive there so we could sometimes hear comments from them. They were all tight away games back then, A trip to Oldham would be tricky, we were never guaranteed the two points anywhere away from home in those days.

Then there was the weather. We played Bramley in the snow one year in the Challenge Cup. They gave us a really good game. We played them again in a night match - the floodlights weren't working properly, there weren't many fans there and the pitch was a muddy slope. This helped level things for the smaller clubs. That doesn't happen today because the dry conditions and good pitches help the bigger clubs run away with games.

I think the other thing that does still happen today is that clubs raise their game because they are playing one of the most famous rugby league clubs in the world, Saints. The nature of the St Helens team throughout the ages has been to throw the ball about. With that style of play, the odd mistake or two is inevitable and that presents opportunities for the opposition.

The coldest game I have ever played in was against Halifax at Thrum Hall. My feet were numb; it made it difficult to kick goals. Another time we played in a friendly at Huddersfield - it started snowing, then raining, and then sleeting, then became very windy. Everybody just wanted to get off the pitch with the exception of Garry Schofield who played with his socks rolled down, his sleeves rolled up and was jogging round like it was spring. After the game, it was difficult to get into the shower because the kit was frozen rigid onto our bodies.

I would say my main strengths as a player were running a good line and feeding my winger. I could read a game well. I also had a good understanding with my wing man. When Eric Hughes was coach, Saints brought union centres Scott Gibbs and Andy Northey to the club. He would set the cones out and have me showing how to run good lines on an angle. They were just straight runners in union. It was funny because he'd have me doing this once a week after training and then later he sold me. I used to enjoy it though because both Scott and Andy were top lads. If it was going to improve the team, I was happy to help them.

I don't think my defence was as good as it should have been, but I felt it improved a lot at Bradford. I never thought that tackling tyres

127

Neil Holding and Paul Loughlin celebrate their induction into the St Helens Past Players Hall of Fame in 2007. (Alex Service)

was going to make me a better tackler. I thought that I could always get Bernard Dwyer or Paul Forber to do all my tackling for me at Saints.

When I was playing, everybody who took the field was a tough opponent. I used to hate playing against small, stocky blokes like Joe Ropati at Warrington. His legs were massive and because he was close to the ground he was difficult to tackle. Small, fast players were always tricky too. I remember the loose-forward at Salford, Mick McTigue - he could snap a player in his half with his defence. In those days, a smack round the chops was part and parcel of the game. Playing on small grounds against aggressive teams was always tough. That's another reason it was good playing at Saints, there were gaps there and I could run off.

I hope I always remembered the fans. I'll never forget my dad telling me you can be the best or worst player in the world but if you're nice to people then they'll not forget that.

Paddy Loughlin

"Paul had some good times and made great friends that he will never forget. Paul's always stuck by the advice I gave him about the fans. People come up to me and say that Paul's a cracking lad and that's not because of me. How many kids listen to what their dads tell them, not a great many. Paul did though. It started in The Rifle when a young girl asked Paul for his autograph. I explained to him that his picture was probably all over her bedroom wall and that to her, he was like a film star. She paid to watch him play. It doesn't take anything to be nice and he's always been like that."

The game has changed so much today. It is miles faster than it used to be, the players are much fitter. I don't think they are as skilful as players used to be though, it seems to be more athletic and power-based now. I think the Australians still have it right because all their players are still very skilful, but still have the power too. The Kiwis are the same. I don't think the forward game has changed that much. I just think the style of play these days seems a bit more robotic. There aren't so many moves from the scrum. Saints are probably the exception. They still use the move where they pass the ball behind a couple of players' backs, missing them out. It still works and they score a lot of tries with that. We used to call it the 'piss off'. If the ball was going in front, it was called 'face me'. Like Alex Murphy says, it's basic rugby league, it's easy.

I would never really have much to eat before a game, something light like beans on toast. I would drink plenty of water to keep myself hydrated but if a player had too much, it would make them sick.

I'm doing different things to keep fit now that I've retired from rugby. I am now a goalkeeper for Garswood FC. I took my son to play there and found out they had a veterans' team. One of the coaches asked me if I fancied a game as their goalkeeper was packing it in. They knew I could catch the ball so gave me a go. I've been playing for five years now and I really enjoy it. It's great to have the craic of the dressing room and a drink afterwards.

Team mates at Bradford Bulls and St Helens. With Bernard at the Saints Past Players Annual Dinner in 2005. (Alex Service)

A former workmate of mine called Fran tried to make me an internet superstar by uploading a video of me dancing to *California Dreamin'* onto YouTube. He was filming it on his phone while I was messing about. He told me he was going to put it on YouTube, but at the time, I had no idea what that was. When he showed me, I thought my moves were quite good. Nobody's approached me about celebrity dancing yet, but surely it's only a matter of time.

When I was injured, I also used to enjoy doing the summarising on Hospital Radio or Radio Merseyside with Alan Rooney. I also did a couple of match videos with Saints match video commentator Ron 'Halan Unte' Hoofe. It never bothered me if I had to deal with the press, once I got used to it, it was fine. I was never really interviewed that much anyway. I knew what I was talking about.

Paddy Loughlin

"One funny memory is Saints writer Bill Bates asking Paul, 'I believe you are a twin, which one of you is oldest?' Paul replied, 'Me, by 12 months'. I always told Paul not to make an enemy of anybody writing in the paper."

Steve Prescott is an inspiration to everyone in rugby league and outside the game. Since being diagnosed with his devastating and rare stomach cancer he had raised money for charity and run marathons. Bad things always seem to happen to the nicest people. He's a top bloke and was a good player. He was probably another local lad who didn't get what he asked for contract-wise and ended up moving on to play for Hull and Wakefield.

I played in a game of wheelchair rugby for his foundation. I was part of a team of former professional players against the England Wheelchair Rugby team. The game was at Widnes. One of our former forwards came to play too. We had a practice in the chairs before the match and we were OK going forward but when it came to going backwards, I just ended up doing circles. I was dizzy from spinning around. The wheelchair team hammered us.

Part of the game is barging into the opposition, one young lad barged into one of our former forwards. Uh oh. He didn't like it and had an angry look on his face. He looked at me and shook his head, this was going to get ugly. The next time the lad got the ball our forward stiff-armed him, clocked him around the head. I said to him, "You can't do that, the lad's disabled." I told him he should apologise. He walked up to the lad, ruffled his hair and gruffly said, "Now, are you alright? It's a tough game this rugby, lad." The kid was in tears. He can always say he was stiff-armed by a certain Saints legend, he's in good and famous company there. But it was stooping a bit low, literally.

I was going to be a part of a boxing event for the foundation but my chosen opponent Phil Veivers refused to get his belly out. Brian McDermott put himself forward but, quite frankly, he's a former boxer and a former Marine so if anyone thinks I would fight him, they're mad. I had originally agreed as long as I didn't have to fight Tim Street and so I had selected Phil Veivers as an opponent. What Phil didn't know was that I have been in serious boxing training for some time. When he found out he pulled out. He said he was too old and his belly was too fat which I told him suited me. He had only originally agreed to fight me after we discussed it when playing snooker after about nine pints. The way he was talking then he sounded like he was an Australian boxing champion.

Phil Veivers

"My first impression of meeting Paul was that he was this gangly kid with a little head, he had a moustache that reminded me of a cricket match, eleven either side.

As a person, if he was any more laid back, he'd be asleep. He's a great bloke though and he was best man at my wedding and I wouldn't do that if I didn't think much of him. He's a loyal guy and a comedian who loves a laugh and a joke.

He was pretty much the ultimate winger's centre, the best you could possibly have. Just ask some of the blokes who played on the wing with him – ask Les or Sully how many tries he put them in for. He probably made a lot more tries than he scored.

It was a laugh a minute working on the ground with him. He's six feet odd, 15 stones and yet it was fantastic to see how terrified he was of mice. One of the funniest memories of working on the ground with him was the time he'd just come back from a double hernia operation. Neil and I got some rope ready and informed him we would tie him up on the pitch. I've never seen a man run... well, hobble... so fast in my life. We couldn't stop laughing. We got him, tied him up and left him in the middle of the pitch for everyone in the restaurant to see.

Then there was the time Neil put a big rat in a jar of coffee so its head and front paws were facing out. We asked Lockers to brew up, off he went to boil the kettle and get the cups out. He opened the coffee jar to come face to face with the rat. Well, the jar ended up in the air and the rat was left in the middle of the floor. Lockers was down the players' tunnel at this point trying to get away from us.

It was a little strange coaching him at Huddersfield with him being a mate, especially as we used to travel over together. Having said that, Paul always knew when it was time to work and when it was time to be a mate.

As for him claiming that I wouldn't face him in the boxing ring, ask him how many broken ribs he has? He wouldn't fight me when I was 30. He waited until I was 46 going on 47 with me having had broken ribs throughout my career. He said there would be no head shots too and he asked me when we'd had a drink. He's very brave with some beer inside him. At the end of the day, there's only one guy with brains and that's me."

I have done Boxercise training for five years at Wigan Boxing Club. It's owned by former Olympic boxer John Lyon who works at a different Pilkington's factory from the one I do. The daughter of player I used to play against, Geoff Dean who played for Trafford and Prescot, used to be a boxer. Adele and her husband Lee got the training going. A friend of mine started doing the training and said I should try it. I had just finished playing and needed to do something to keep me fit, it's been fantastic and has probably took at least a stone off me. Paul Sculthorpe and some of the current Wigan squad go too. I wish I had done it during my playing days, I might have laid out a few. I can recommend it to people because it keeps you fit and really gets your stomach muscles going.

I used to play cricket for the Radio Lollipop Charity and was even once described as a pace bowler. Well I thought I was fast anyway. A couple of other Saints players played too. Paul Forber could have been an Ian Botham, he could bowl at pace. We played at Woodford Cricket Club in Manchester. Forber hit about 12 sixes that day. I had previously played at school and really enjoyed it. West Park always had a good cricket side. I still love watching cricket to this day.

I played in a Great Britain versus Australia rugby league legends match at Widnes, there were great players on either side, including Mal Meninga, playing. Without a doubt, the Hulme brothers were taking the match far more seriously than all of the other players. They were still tackling people hard. They'll probably still be doing that when they are 70. Those games always start of as a bit of fun, but when you see the big forwards charging into each other, there still can be injuries. There is still pride in those games. There was also some good skill on show at the game as well.

I packed in my playing career because I had been taken on at Pilkington's glass factory in St Helens as a machine operator. It was a four month temporary contract but at the time of writing I have been there for 10 years. I don't think some of the lads there can believe they are working alongside me. Many of them touch me in the morning when I come to work because they can't believe they are working with the legend.

They don't even mind when I nick all the coffee, milk and sugar. Chris Gill, who works there and put me in touch with the co-writer of this book, even comes and practises his tackling technique on me every morning although I put him right. There are some good lads there, some former rugby players, some football players - there's even a couple of Wiganers there, but you can't have everything. It's a good place to work and we all have a good laugh. I realise how lucky I am to work at such a good place in this day and age. It was hard for me at first because I had never worked in a factory before, but everybody gets on with each other.

I decided to do this book because I can't wait to read it myself. There are so many tales looking back, it will be good to have them all in one place. I know a lot of it sounds like we messed about a lot, but there was a lot of hard training too. People might read it and reminisce a bit because they might have forgotten what it was like in the 1980s.

A lot of Saints fans have fixations on the teams of the 1960s, the 1970s and the Super League era, so it's nice to be able to talk about the side we had in the 1980s and early 1990s. It wasn't as glamorous for us as it has been for the team in recent years and the club didn't spend as much money. Having said that, we did have some world class players then. Going back to the selection of the greatest ever Saints XVII put together in 2010. Harry Pinner from our era would have been in there for me. He was a Great Britain captain after all. Hopefully, this book might help to redress the balance a little and remind people there were some good players in my era. There was a Saints before Super League. I would find it very difficult to pick a best

134

ever XIII I played with or against, but have always said that Shane Cooper and Kevin Ward would be in it.

Shane kept the side going through the barren years. He was a fantastic organiser and we could go somewhere with half a team and he would still lead from the front. He was brilliant to play alongside for me as a centre with his passing from stand-off or as a loose-forward.

As for Kevin Ward, he was just a legend. He had those great years at Castleford and Manly, and for Great Britain. When he came to Saints, he was immense. Not only did he stand out, but he helped bring players on such as Bernard Dwyer and Jon Neill. They played really well trying to match up to him. He was a good laugh too, even though he still calls me Tom.

Chris Arkwright was another hero of mine too. If it hadn't been for injury, he could have made more international appearances than anyone at St Helens.

But I'd like to be remembered as a skilful, fair player. I really enjoyed it at Saints; I had the time of my life. I had the injuries and a couple of setbacks, and without them maybe I could have even done better. Coaching isn't for me though.

Paddy Loughlin

"I always thought he could have broken Kel Coslett's record at Saints and if it hadn't been for the two broken arms, I think he would have done. He might have even been the closest to get to Neil Fox's record."

I always wanted to be an Eric Ashton type centre – a graceful player who would put his winger away. I never once thought I'd be a Saints player, but I got my chance and took it. I really enjoyed it and hopefully I made a few people smile along the way. I've also made loads of good friends playing rugby and had some great laughs. It was hard work sometimes, but it wasn't all hard work as you will now have realised.

Appendix: Statistics and records

Representative matches

Great Britain

14+1 appearances from 1988 to 1992 (11 @ centre, 3 @ full-back, 1 sub)
2 tries, 31 goals, 70 points
Won 9 lost 5
Played against:
Australia 5   New Zealand 4
France 4   Papua New Guinea 2

Opponents	Date	Result	Scored	Position
France (a)	24/1/1988	28–14	3g	Centre
Papua New Guinea (a, WC)	22/5/1988	42–22	7g	Full-back
Australia (a)	11/6/1988	6–17	1g	Full-back
Australia (a)	28/6/1988	14–34	3g	Full-back
Australia (a, WC)	9/7/1988	26–12	3g	Centre
New Zealand (a, WC)	17/7/1988	10–12	1t, 1g	Centre
France (h)	21/1/1989	26–10	3g	Centre
New Zealand (h)	21/10/1989	16–24	2g	Centre
New Zealand (h)	28/10/1989	26–6	5g	Centre
New Zealand (h, WC)	11/11/1989	10–6	1g	Centre
France (a)	18/3/1990	8–4		Centre
Australia (h) (sub)	10/11/1990	10–14	1t	Sub for Offiah
France (h)	16/2/1991	60–4		Centre
Papua New Guinea (a)	31/5/1992	20–14	2g	Centre
Australia (a)	12/6/1992	6–22		Centre

Great Britain tour matches (excluding tests)

1988:
Australia 5+1 appearances, 23 goals
New Zealand 1+1 appearances, 5 goals

1992:
Papua New Guinea 1 appearance, 4 goals
Australia: 1+1 appearances, 1 goal

Great Britain Colts and under-21s

Colts: 2 appearances against France in 1984-85
Under-21s: 2 appearances against France in 1986-87

Lancashire

2 appearances from 1988 to 1989 (Both @ centre)
3 goals
Lost 2 against Yorkshire

Opponents	Date	Result	Scored	Position
Yorkshire	21/9/1988	14–24	1g	Centre
Yorkshire	20/9/1989	12–56	2g	Centre

Clubs

St Helens
286+11 appearances from 1984 to 1995
80 tries, 842 goals, 2,008 points

Honours
Challenge Cup: Runners-up 1986–87, 1988–89, 1990–91.
John Player Special Trophy: Winners 1987–88,
Premiership: Winners: 1992–93; Runners-up 1987–88, 1991–92

Season	App	Sub	Tries	Goals	Points
1983–84	1	2	0	2	4
1984–85	2	2	0	5	10
1985–86	24	3	4	43	102
1986–87	39	0	9	178	392
1987–88	37	1	8	111	254
1988–89	33	0	5	109	238
1989–90	32	0	17	135	338
1990–91	27	0	8	94	220
1991–92	11	0	6	40	104
1992–93	19	1	5	65	150
1993–94	29	0	3	58	128
1994–95	19	2	10	2	44
1995–96	13	0	6	0	24
Totals:	**286**	**11**	**81**	**842**	**2,008**

Bradford Bulls
59+5 appearances from 1995 to 1997
28 tries, 13 goals, 138 points

Honours
Super League: Winners 1997
Challenge Cup: Runners-up 1996, 1997

Season	App	Sub	Tries	Goals	Points
1995–96	7	0	3	1	14
1996	23	3	12	3	54
1997	29	2	13	9	70
Totals:	**59**	**5**	**28**	**13**	**138**

Huddersfield Giants
36+2 appearances from 1998 to 1999
5 tries, 4 goals, 28 points

Season	App	Sub	Tries	Goals	Points
1998	12	1	1	4	12
1999	24	1	4	0	16
Totals:	**36**	**2**	**5**	**4**	**28**

Swinton Lions

Season	App	Sub	Tries	Goals	Points
2000	14	5	7	1	30
2001	10	1	4	1	18
Totals:	**24**	**6**	**11**	**2**	**48**

Career summary

Team	App	Sub	Tries	Goals	Points
Great Britain tests	14	1	2	31	70
Great Britain tour	8	3	0	33	66
Lancashire	2	0	0	3	6
St Helens	286	11	81	842	2,008
Bradford Bulls	59	5	28	13	138
Huddersfield Giants	36	2	5	4	28
Swinton Lions	24	6	11	2	48
Totals:	**429**	**28**	**127**	**928**	**2,364**

Finals

St Helens

Challenge Cup

1986–87

Halifax 19 St Helens 18 (Half-time 12–2)

Halifax: Graham Eadie, Scott Wilson, Colin Whitfield, Grant Rix, Wilf George, Chris Anderson, Gary Stephens, Graham Beevers, Seamus McCallion, Keith Neller, Paul Dixon, Mick Scott, John Pendlebury. Subs: Brian Juliff, Neil James.

Scorers: Tries: George, McCallion, Eadie; Goals: Whitfield (3); Drop-goal: Pendlebury.

St Helens: Phil Veivers, Barry Ledger, Paul Loughlin, Mark Elia, Kevin McCormack, Brett Clark, Neil Holding, Tony Burke, Graham Liptrot, John Fieldhouse, Andy Platt, Roy Haggerty, Chris Arkwright. Subs: Paul Round, Paul Forber (dnp).

Scorers: Tries: Elia, Loughlin, Round; Goals: Loughlin (3).

1988–89

Wigan 27 St Helens 0 (Half-time 12–0)

Wigan: Steve Hampson, Tony Iro, Kevin Iro, Dean Bell,, Joe Lydon, Shaun Edwards, Andy Gregory, Ian Lucas, Nicky Kiss, Adrian Shelford, Andy Platt, Ian Potter, Ellery Hanley. Subs: Denis Betts, Andy Goodway.

Scorers: Tries: Kevin Iro (2), Hanley, Gregory, Hampson. Goals: Lydon (3); Drop-goal: Gregory.

St Helens: Gary Connolly, Michael O'Connor, Phil Veivers, Paul Loughlin, Les Quirk, Shane Cooper, Neil Holding, Tony Burke, Paul Groves, Paul Forber, Bernard Dwyer, Roy Haggerty, Paul Vautin. Subs: Darren Bloor, Stuart Evans.

1990–91

Wigan 13 St Helens 8 (Half-time 12–0)

Wigan: Steve Hampson, David Myers, Kevin Iro, Dean Bell, Frano Botica, Shaun Edwards, Andy Gregory, Ian Lucas, Martin Dermott, Andy Platt, Denis Betts, Phil Clarke, Ellery Hanley. Subs: Bobbie Goulding, Andy Goodway.

Scorers: Tries: Myers, Botica. Goals: Botica (2); Drop-goal: Gregory.

St Helens: Phil Veivers, Alan Hunte, Tea Ropati, Paul Loughlin, Les Quirk, Jonathan Griffiths, Paul Bishop, Jonathan Neill, Bernard Dwyer, Kevin Ward, John Harrison, George Mann, Shane Cooper. Subs: Gary Connolly, Paul Groves.

Scorers: Try: Hunte; Goals: Bishop (2).

138

John Player Special Trophy

1987–88

St Helens 15 Leeds 14 (Half-time 9-14)
St Helens: Phil Veivers, David Tanner, Paul Loughlin, Mark Elia, Les Quirk, Shane Cooper, Neil Holding, Tony Burke, Paul Groves, Peter Souto, Paul Forber, Roy Haggerty, Andy Platt. Subs: David Large (dnp), Stuart Evans.
Scorers: Tries: Loughlin (2). Goals: Loughlin (3); Drop-goal: Holding.
Leeds: Marty Gurr, Steve Morris, Garry Schofield, Peter Jackson, John Basnett, David Creaser, Ray Ashton, Peter Tunks, Colin Maskill, Kevin Rayne, Roy Powell, Paul Medley, David Heron. Subs: Carl Gibson, John Fairbank.
Scorers: Tries: Creasser, Jackson. Goals: Creasser (3).

Premiership

1987-88

Widnes 38 St Helens 14 (Half-time 16-2)
Widnes: Duncan Platt, Rick Thackery, Andy Currier, Darren Wright, Martin Offiah, Barry Dowd, David Hulme, Kurt Sorensen, Phil McKenzie, Joe Grima, Mike O'Neill, Paul Hulme., Richard Eyres. Subs: Alan Tait, Steve O'Neill.
Scorers: Tries: Wright (2), David Hulme (2), Tait, McKenzie, Sorensen. Goals: Currier (4), Platt.
St Helens: Paul Loughlin, Barrie Ledger, David Tanner, Mark Elia, Les Quirk, Mark Bailey, Neil Holding, Tony Burke, Paul Groves, Stuart Evans, Paul Forber, John Fieldhouse, Roy Haggerty. Subs: Shaun Allen, Bernard Dwyer.
Scorers: Tries: Ledger, Haggerty. Goals: Loughlin (3).

1991–92

Wigan 48 St Helens 16 (Half-time 10–12)
Wigan: Steve Hampson, Joe Lydon, Dean Bell, Gene Miles, Martin Offiah, Frano Botica, Shaun Edwards, Neil Cowie, Martin Dermott, Andy Platt, Denis Betts, Billy McGinty, Phil Clarke. Subs: David Myers, Sam Panapa.
Scorers: Tries: Offiah (2), Betts (2), Platt, Myers, Miles. Goals: Botica (10).
St Helens: Phil Veivers, Alan Hunte, Gary Connolly, Paul Loughlin, Anthony Sullivan, Tea Ropati, Paul Bishop, Jonathan Neill, Bernard Dwyer, Kevin Ward, Sonny Nickle, George Mann, Shane Cooper. Subs: Jonathan Griffiths, Paul Groves.
Scorers: Tries: Sullivan (2), Loughlin. Goals: Loughlin (2).

1992–93

St Helens 10 Wigan 4 (Half-time 4-0)
St Helens: David Lyon, Mike Riley, Gary Connolly, Paul Loughlin, Alan Hunte, Tea Ropati, Gus O'Donnell, Jonathan Neill, Bernard Dwyer, George Mann, Chris Joynt, Sonny Nickle, Shane Cooper. Subs: Jonathan Griffiths, Phil Veivers.
Scorers: Tries: Connolly, Loughlin. Drop-goals: O'Donnell (2).
Wigan: Paul Atcheson, Jason Robinson, Sam Panapa, Andrew Farrar, martin Offiah, Frano Botica, Shaun Edwards, Neil Cowie, Martin Dermott, Kelvin Skerrett, Mick Cassidy, Andrew Farrell, Phil Clarke. Subs: Mike Forshaw, Ian Gildart.
Scorer: Try: Forshaw.

Bradford Bulls

Challenge Cup

1996

St Helens 40 Bradford Bulls 32 (Half-time 12–14)

St Helens: Steve Prescott, Danny Arnold, Scott Gibbs, Paul Newlove, Anthony Sullivan, Karle Hammond, Bobbie Goulding, Apollo Perelini, Keiron Cunningham, Andy Leatham, Chris Joynt, Simon Booth, Andy Northey. Subs: Tommy Martyn, Ian Pickavance, Vila Matautia, Alan Hunte.

Scorers: Tries: Prescott (2), Arnold (2), Cunningham, Booth, Pickavance, Perelini. Goals: Goulding (4).

Bradford Bulls: Nathan Graham, Paul Cook, Matt Calland, Paul Loughlin, Jon Scales, Graeme Bradley, Robbie Paul, Brian McDermott, Bernard Dwyer, Jon Hamer, Jeremy Donougher, Sonny Nickle, Simon Knox. Subs: Karl Fairbank, Paul Medley, Jason Donohue, Carlos Hassan.

Scorers: Tries: Paul (3), Scales, Dwyer. Goals: Cook (6)

1997

St Helens 32 Bradford Bulls 22 (Half-time 16–10)

St Helens: Steve Prescott, Danny Arnold, Andy Haigh, Paul Newlove, Anthony Sullivan, Tommy Martyn, Bobbie Goulding, Apollo Perelini, Keiron Cunningham, Julian O'Neill, Chris Joynt, Derek McVey, Karle Hammond. Subs: Ian Pickavance, Vila Matautia, Andy Northey, Chris Morley.

Scorers: Tries: Martyn (2), Hammond, Joynt, Sullivan. Goals: Goulding (6).

Bradford Bulls: Stuart Spruce, Abi Ekoku, Danny Peacock, Paul Loughlin, Paul Cook, Graeme Bradley, Robbie Paul, Brian McDermott, James Lowes, Tahi Reihana, Sonny Nickle, Bernard Dwyer, Steve McNamara. Subs: Paul Medley, Matt Calland, Glen Tomlinson, Simon Knox.

Scorers: Tries: Peacock, Loughlin, Tomlinson, Lowes. Goals: McNamara (3).

All Local Lads

St Helens and Pilkington Recs
Rugby League Football Club

Includes St Helens Recs Football Club 1898 to 1913

ALEX SERVICE and DENIS WHITTLE

All Local Lads is the complete history of St Helens and Pilkington Recs, including their early days in rugby union, then in association football, and their time as the only ever works team in professional rugby league between the wars. There is also full coverage and interviews of their post-war time in amateur rugby league up to 2008. Published in 2008 at £13.95, now available at just £10.00 post free direct from London League Publications Ltd. Credit card orders via www.llpshop.co.uk , orders by cheque to LLP, PO Box 65784, London NW2 9NS

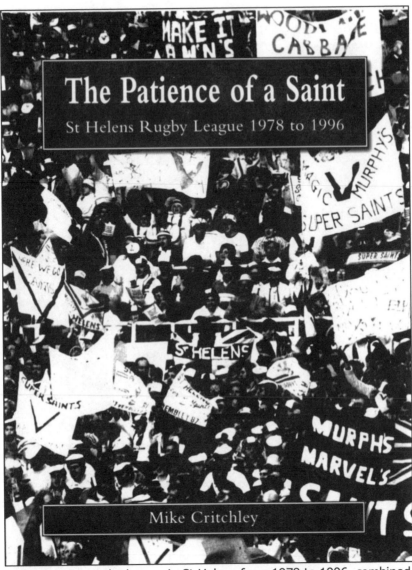

The Patience of a Saint

St Helens Rugby League 1978 to 1996

Mike Critchley

Reflections on rugby league in St Helens from 1978 to 1996, combined with growing up in the town and the changes during that time.
Special offer – order direct from London League Publications Ltd for just £5.00 post free.
Credit card orders via www.llpshop.co.uk ,
orders by cheque to LLP, PO Box 65784, London NW2 9NS

Best in the Northern Union

The pioneering 1910 Rugby League Lions tour of Australia and New Zealand

Tom Mather

Fascinating account of the first Great Britain Lions tour of Australia and New Zealand. Published in 2010 at £12.95, special offer £12.00 direct from London League Publications Ltd. Credit card orders via www.llpshop.co.uk , orders by cheque to LLP, PO Box 65784, London NW2 9NS

The King of Brilliance
James Lomas – A Rugby League superstar

By Graham Morris

Comprehensive biography of one of the game's great players from the Northern Union days. James Lomas was the sport's leading player before the First World War and captained the 1910 tourists to Australia and New Zealand. To be published in October 2011 @ £16.95 (hardback).
Order direct from London League Publications Ltd. Credit card orders via www.llpshop.co.uk ,
orders by cheque to LLP, PO Box 65784, London NW2 9NS

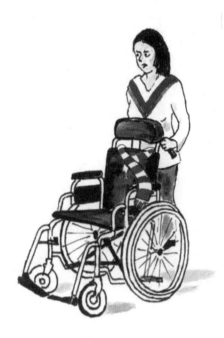

Braver than all the rest
A mother fights for her son

Philip Howard

Dave and Sarah Burgess are devastated when their young son Karl is found to have muscular dystrophy. Then another tragedy hits the family hard. But the family are committed to do the best they can for Karl, who has a passion for rugby league. Based in Castleton, a Yorkshire town near the border with Lancashire, Karl's determination to get the most out of life, despite his disability, inspires those around him, in particular Chris Anderton, one of the Castleton Rugby League Club players.

Philip Howard is a retired teacher who had responsibility for special needs at a sixth form college. He is a lifelong rugby league fan from St Helens, but now lives near Hull. This is his first novel.

Published in September 2010 at £9.95. Available direct from London League Publications Ltd for just £9.00 post free. For credit card payments visit www.llpshop.co.uk , cheque payments to PO Box 65784, London NW2 9NS, payable to London League Publications Ltd. It can also be ordered from any bookshop for £9.95 (ISBN: 9781903659526).

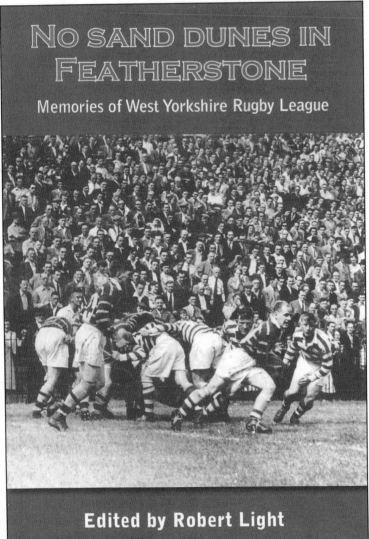

NO SAND DUNES IN FEATHERSTONE

Memories of West Yorkshire Rugby League

Edited by Robert Light

Based on the *'Up and Under'* University of Huddersfield oral history project, this book includes memories from players, coaches, club officials, referees, journalists and supporters from the First World War to the present. Every rugby league supporter will enjoy this fascinating book. Published in October 2010 at £12.95. Available direct from London League Publications Ltd for just £12.00. For credit card payments visit www.llpshop.co.uk , cheque payments to PO Box 65784, London NW2 9NS, cheques payable to London League Publications Ltd. It can also be ordered from any bookshop for £12.95 (ISBN: 9781903659533).